THE LION CHILDREN

The story of a journey that started in the Cotswold Hills

and led to living

with lions in the

Okavango Delta.

This journey has

only just begun.

THE LION CHILDREN

Written by Travers, Angus
and Maisie McNeice with Oakley
between November 1999 and January 2001

ORION

To Mum and Pieter,
Dad and Cindy and our sister Emily

In memory of Corrie

First published in Great Britain in 2001 by Orion
An imprint of Orion Books Ltd
Orion House, 5 Upper St Martin's Lane, London WC2H 9EA

The right of Angus, Maisie and Travers McNeice
to be identified as the authors of this work
has been asserted by them in accordance with
the Copyright, Designs and Patents Act 1988.

All illlustrations are by Masie and Angus
with the exception of those by Oakley on pages 105 and 131.

Pictures on page 162/3 © Carla Signorini Jones
Page 52/3, Page 78 and Page 172/3 © David Keith Jones
Supplied by Images of Africa Photobank

A CIP catalogue record for this book
is available from the British Library

ISBN 0 75284 160 2

Printed and bound in Italy by Printer Trento S.r.l.

CONTENTS

FOREWORD

THIS IS AN ASTONISHING BOOK, by an even more astonishing trio of children. It's hard to describe: you have to read it, and once you start reading you can't stop. Think of *Swallows and Amazons*, except that this story is true and it all happens far from the comfort of England. Think of *The Lion, the Witch and the Wardrobe*, except that the Lion Children need no magic wardrobe to pass through; no fake world of wonder. The real Africa, humanity's cradle, is more magical than anything C S Lewis could dream up. And, while they have no witch, these young authors do have a most remarkable mother. More of her in a moment.

Travers, Angus, Maisie and family have lived under canvas for almost as long as their little brother Oakley (think of *Just William*) can remember. All three of them have been driving Land Rovers ever since their feet could reach the pedals, and changing tyres (frequently) for as long as they've been strong enough to lift them. They are self-sufficient and trustworthy far beyond their years, yet not in that disagreeable sense of being streetwise and fly. Field Marshall Montgomery once described Mao Tse Tung as the sort of man you could go into the jungle with. Well, I'm not sure I'd go with Mao Tse Tung into Hyde Park, but I would unhesitatingly go into the jungle with Travers, Angus and Maisie, and no adult companions at all. No gun, just quick-witted young people with clear eyes, fast reflexes and most of a lifetime (albeit a short one) of African know-how. I don't know what to do if I meet an elephant. They do. I'm terrified of puff adders, mambas and scorpions. They take them in their stride. At the same time, dependable and strong as they are, they still bubble with the innocence and charm of youth. This is still *Swallows and Amazons*, still an idyll, the sort of childhood that for most of us exists only in dreams and idealised misrememberings, the land of lost content. Yet it is firmly in the real world. These innocents have seen favourite lions brutally killed, have rapped out reports of such tragedies in the dispassionate argot of the radio link, have assisted at the subsequent postmortems.

This accomplished book is entirely the work of its young authors, but it isn't hard to guess the source of their *ability* to do it – their imagination, their enterprise, their unorthodoxy, their adventurous spirit. My wife and I first met Kate Nicholls in 1992 when she was living in the Cotswolds, pregnant with Oakley, commuting to study in Oxford libraries. A successful actress, she had become disillusioned with the stage and developed, in her late thirties, a passion (passion is the story of her life) for the science of evolution. Kate doesn't do anything by halves and, for her, an interest in evolution meant deep immersion in libraries, digging up the original research literature. With only minimal guidance from me in what became a series of informal tutorials, her reading transformed her into something of a scholarly authority on Darwinian theory. Her eventual decision to pull up roots and head for Botswana, where Darwinism can be daily witnessed in *practice*, seemed entirely in character: a natural, if unconventional extension of the same scholarly quest. Her children, one can't help feeling, have a pretty fortunate inheritance, as well as an almost unique environment in which to realise it.

They also have to thank their mother for their education, and this is perhaps the most surprising aspect of their life. Quite soon after arriving in Botswana, Kate decided to teach them herself. A brave decision, I think I would have counselled against it. But I would have been wrong. Although all their schooling is done in camp they keep proper terms, have challenging homework assignments, and work towards internationally accredited exams. Kate gets good results by standard educational certifications, while at the same time tending, indeed enhancing, the natural sense of wonder that normal children too often lose during their teens. I don't think any reader of these pages could fail to judge her unorthodox School in the Bush a brilliant success. The proof lies in the book, for, to repeat, the children and they alone wrote it. All three authors show themselves to be excellent writers: sensitive, literate, articulate, intelligent and creative. Having taught at Oxford for thirty years I say that any university will be fortunate to receive an application from any one of them.

Kate's choice of Botswana rather than anywhere else in Africa was fortuitous. In the fullness of time it led to her meeting Pieter Kat ("I'm going to be Katy Kat, can you *bear* it?"). And of course the lions – wild lions, living and dying in the world for which the natural selection of their ancestors had prepared them. Pieter – reserved, yet warm and confident, the best sort of strong, silent man – complements Kate perfectly. Kate is warm and strong but in a very different way, seldom silent, never reserved, always passionate, occasionally infuriating. Pieter is the ideal stepfather for her children, and these young scientists have in turn become an indispensable part of the lion research and conservation project.

It wasn't till last year that my family and I finally visited the camp. The experience was unforgettable, and I can testify to the picture painted in these pages. It really is just like that: more wonderful than mad, but a bit of both. My daughter Juliet went out ahead, part of a large invasion of young visitors who soon picked up the enthusiasm of the resident family. On Juliet's first full day in Africa, Travers took her out in a Land Rover, tracking radio-collared lions. When we received Juliet's letter home, brimming with excitement at such an initiation, I relayed the story to her grandmother, who interrupted me with panic in her voice: "Plus, of course, at least two armed African rangers?" I had to confess that Travers really had been Juliet's only companion, that he had been driving the Land Rover all by himself, and that as far as I knew the camp boasted neither African rangers nor arms. I don't mind admitting that, though I concealed it from my mother, I was pretty anxious about the story myself. But that was before I had seen Travers in the bush. Or, indeed, Angus or Maisie.

We arrived a month after Juliet, and our fears were soon put to rest. I had been to Africa before, indeed was born there. But I have never felt so close to the wild.

Or so close to lions or any large wild animals. And there was the marvellous camaraderie of life in camp; laughter and argument in the dining tent, everybody shouting at once. I think of sleeping and waking amid the sounds of the African night, the untiring "Work harder" of the Cape Turtle Dove, the insolently robust barking of the baboons, the distant – and sometimes not so distant – roaring of the prides. I think of Juliet's sixteenth birthday party timed for the full moon: a surreal scene of candlelit table standing proud and alone on open ground, miles from camp and indeed from anywhere else; of the catch in the throat as we watched the huge moon rising exactly on cue, first reflected in the shallow Jackal Pan and later picking out the spectral shapes of marauding hyenas – which had us hastily bundling the sleeping Oakley into the safety of the Land Rover. I think of our last night and a dozen lions, gnawing and growling on a recently killed zebra only just outside the camp. The atavistic emotions that this primitive night scene aroused – for, whatever our upbringing, our genes are African – haunt me still.

But I can't begin to do justice to this world which has been the setting for such an extraordinary childhood. I was only there for a week, and I am no doubt jaded with maturity. Read the book and experience, through watchful young eyes, all Africa – and her prodigies.

RICHARD DAWKINS

INTRODUCTION

TRAVERS

ONE SATURDAY MORNING in July 2000 I awoke as the sun peered through the shade-cloth window of my canvas meru tent. On a weekend morning I would usually lie in bed and read, but today I wanted to go on a game drive by myself in order to think peacefully. The mornings are cold during the African winter so I dressed warmly and walked up the sand path to the kitchen. On the way I watched an elephant browsing in the distance. Our kitchen is just a canvas fly-sheet held up by poles and has open sides and reed mats on the floor. With a sinking heart I saw that the kitchen had been raided during the night. The place looked as though a bomb had hit it. Broken pieces of china were everywhere, the rubbish had been scattered across the floor. As I started to pick it up I noticed that the tin of hot chocolate had been bitten through by a pair of long canines. The tracks in the sand showed me that a hyena had come in the night. I sighed because I knew this would mean many nights awake persuading the dangerous predator to stay clear of our camp. I found a tin bowl the hyena had not got his paws on and poured myself some cereal. I ate it quickly, looked at the mess again and selfishly decided to leave the chaos for someone else to clear up.

As I got into our green Land Rover pickup I checked that the binoculars were with me and I drove out of camp. I am sixteen and have been driving for five years – my Mother taught me. I decided to go on a quick twenty-kilometre drive, known to us as Steenbok Loop. There was quite a lot of game out that morning: impalas, zebras, elephants and a few giraffes. As I drove up to a termite mound I saw a young lioness. She was lying on her back catching the first rays of the early morning sun. I have known her almost all her life and have grown to understand her story and love her. I watched as she slowly moved off into the acacia forest to find some shade and then I headed back to camp. I had been out for an hour and a half, and people might start to wonder where I was.

On arriving home I was greeted by my youngest brother Oakley, who raced me to the kitchen. He is only six years old but runs faster than most people in camp. The rest of the family was sitting around the table drinking coffee and laughing, and I went to join them for a while before going on to fix tyres, my special treat. Two cars went out yesterday and got punctures, so it was going to take me hours to get things repaired. Everyone was pleased to hear that I had found Freixenet, the young lioness, and we set about planning the rest of the day's activities. We help our mother and stepfather research lions in the Okavango Delta of Botswana… but hang on a second, it has not always been like this. Let me start at the beginning.

There are five of us: Emily (22), Angus (14), Maisie (12), Oakley (6) and me, Travers. Emily and Oaks are actually our half-sister and brother, but to us that

makes no difference. In 1994 we were all still living in England, in our jumbly house in the Cotswolds. Hollybush Cottage was where we all spent our babyhood and a lot of our early childhood. The house is nearly three hundred years old and a perfect example of a classic English country cottage; it has massive apple and plum orchards, lovely gardens, flagstone floors and a big indoor fireplace that always smoked the house out! There is a huge aga in the kitchen, which warmed up the whole house, and there are lots of cosy bedrooms littered all over the place including one in the attic which was mine. As I am writing, my mind fills up with memories that I had long forgotten and that are hard to piece together.

In those days we were all still very little; Oakley, then aged one and a bit, was still in nappies. We lived a very simple, safe and privileged family life. In the summer Mum used to walk us up the lane and read us our bedtime stories on the bench by the village church. We would collect the warm chicken eggs in the morning from the chicken hut and in the evening help Mum pull out carrots and potatoes from her vegetable garden for supper.

Maisie and Angus went to the local primary school, just up the hill from the cottage and Emily went to Chipping Campden Comprehensive. Because I was dyslexic I went to Bruern Abbey, a visionary school at nearby Stow-on-the-Wold. Oaks pottered around at home, playing with the cats in the garden and was glued to Mum's breast twenty-four hours a day. Exciting day trips for us were either going swimming at Splash or going to the local fair.

As we were growing up Dad's career as an actor was taking off and this meant that he was away from home a lot. Mum had given up acting a few years before and started to study biology. Whilst all this was going on Mum and Dad drifted apart, although they still lived together as friends in Hollybush.

One morning, sitting round the kitchen table next to the aga, Mum asked if we would like to go and live in Africa and experience a new way of life. Dad was going to move to Los Angeles and Mum felt ready for a radical change. She didn't like the way things were going in the First World. Children were losing their power as a result of having to live in an increasingly complex technological society; she wanted us to meet new challenges as a family and to learn how to do things for ourselves. In England we turned to experts to do everything for us; once we even abandoned our house and called in the Rat Man, all because Mum saw a rodent in the kitchen.

She got out an atlas of the world and pointed to a country called Botswana and told us about the Okavango Delta and the Kalahari Desert. I had never even heard of the country before that morning; everyone else got very excited, except for me. I was quite scared by the whole concept, but I thought that it was another one of Mum's crazy ideas so I didn't worry too much. It turned out that it was not just an idea but a reality, as two weeks after our talk Mum and Oakley (who was still latched on to Mum's breast) boarded a flight to Botswana and travelled the country looking for a home. When they got back to Hollybush they

showed everyone photographs, which of course I refused to look at, and Mum went on about how she had found an interesting town called Maun very close to the Okavango Delta.

It took us six months to get prepared and as the days drew on I got more and more nervous; fear struck on the day we were leaving. Mum wasn't going to change her mind and stay at home; we were going to move to Africa. I hadn't believed that I would really need to pack, so I quickly threw things in my bag, while crying tears that seemed never ending. Finally we all got on the plane and I was once again reassured that if any one of us were unhappy living in Africa we would return home after a year. This was comforting, as none of us could know quite what this new life would mean to us.

In this book Angus, Maisie and I are going to tell you our story. It evolved out of an English project that Mum set us in school, sitting around the kitchen table in camp. In each chapter we will describe a different stage of our shared journey, each of us from our own perspective. In telling our story we want to help people overcome their fears of the unknown, which is rich coming from me, as I'm the one in the family who has always hated change the most. Also we want to make people aware of this last remaining wilderness, and thereby we hope to help preserve it. And last, but not least, we want to share what we have learned about the lions. They constantly surprise us, fascinate us, challenge us and enchant us. As they play such an important part in our lives, they will play a huge part in this book.

Five years on and Botswana is now our home, England seems so far away. It is ironic that I, the one that least wanted to move, have found my heart belongs to Africa.

ZAMBIA

ZIMBABWE

NAMIBIA

BOTSWANA

SOUTH AFRICA

Maun by Angus

CHAPTER ONE **A DIFFERENT CONTINENT**

THUSO – OUR FIRST
HOUSE IN AFRICA

MAISIE

I REMEMBER PACKING UP to leave England one sunny day in May and Mum saying, 'No sorry darling, you can't take this, and you can't take that.' Then loading all our bags full of books and clothes and the few treasures we could squeeze into the corners. We said goodbye to everyone. The hardest person to say goodbye to was my Dad. He had moved to America a few months before and I didn't know when I would see him next, but as things turned out he came to stay with us for Christmas in Africa. We took one last look at Hollybush, the house that had been my home for all of my seven years, and drove off to the airport, drowning in tears of sadness and joy. Leaving with Mum, Emily, Travers, Angus and Oakley to start our new life in Africa was terrifying, because I didn't know if I would like my new home, but it was also exciting as the prospect of living in Africa felt like such an adventure.

We finally got to the airport, and our grandmother and one of Mum's best friends and her many children came to see us off. They helped with our bags, and after many kisses and goodbyes we left. I was so excited and did not know what to expect next. Mum and Oakley had been to Botswana a few months before to sort out things like school and somewhere for us to live. Mum had told us all about seeing animals roaming free and we could not wait to go.

After a twelve-hour flight we landed in Gaborone, Botswana's capital. Travers had spent the entire flight trying not to be sick. Oakley, then aged one and three-quarters, had disappeared as usual and was found chatting to a family from Pakistan. Emily, Angus and I had been up since dawn straining to see our first glimpse of Africa. As we got off the plane a blast of hot air hit us in the face and the first thing I did when we arrived at the hotel hours later was to dive into the

swimming pool. While I was lying by the pool I saw some huge rocks and I called to Angus to come and explore with me. We looked under every stone and piece of bark, trying to find pieces of 'Africa'. A man came up to us and kindly told us to be careful of scorpions. At which point we were both filled with curiosity and tried to find one.

The next day we drove off in a hired four-wheel-drive car to our new home-town, Maun, right at the bottom of the Okavango Delta. It was a long, ten-hour drive, but we were all too interested to be tired. On the side of the road we saw our first African animal, a dead cow with hundreds of vultures ripping it apart. We made Mum stop so we could look at them. Oakley burst into tears, it was the first dead animal he had ever seen, 'Big ow Mama, big ow cow,' he sobbed.

We stopped briefly in a small village called Nata on the edge of the Kalahari Desert. We were all fascinated, as this was the first African village we had been in. The houses were made of mud and the dilapidated roofs were thatched. On the side of the road a woman was selling little fruits in baskets. The fruits looked like raisins but we found they were chewier than raisins and not so sweet. We drank cold coke and shared our biscuits with the many children that gathered around us. After we left no one spoke for at least half an hour, then Travers broke the silence and said, 'It's just like *Blue Peter*, only real.' We all knew what he meant.

As dusk fell and we started to get sleepy, Emily suddenly pointed ahead and shouted, 'Look, look those things, those things with the necks, those things with the long necks.' She was too thrilled to think straight, and now we really knew we were in Africa as three giraffes ambled across the road in front of us. After that our eyes were peeled and we saw kudus, gemsboks and something else that looked like a cow with a huge dewlap hanging from its neck; the sighting bellowed up huge excitement and we argued about what it was for hours. We later learned it was an eland, the largest antelope in the world.

Finally we got to Maun. I was shocked to see people living in such small mud huts, so closely packed together. I was shocked to see donkeys eating cardboard boxes while hobbling along with their two front feet tied together. I was shocked to see little kids ripping open rubbish bags and eating from them. It was not what I thought it would be like. It was the antithesis of the comfortable Cotswold village I had left behind. Over the five years we've been here Maun has developed very rapidly: in the centre there are more shops and small businesses, but the outskirts of the town remain unchanged.

We stayed in a hotel for a week, as we needed to buy a car, and what a disaster that was – it broke down continuously. We also had to scrub and paint the house that Mum had rented for us, as none of her requests to make the house homely for our arrival had been carried out, and we found that it was filthy. Thuso was a round-house with a large, beautiful garden, filled with orange and lemon trees. We had been warned that the garden also housed several spitting cobras. These large snakes spit their venom into your eyes and you have to wash it out immediately with milk, water or urine (if that's all you have to hand). Angus and I were eager to see a snake but Travers and Mum weren't so enthusiastic.

At last we were ready to move in. We had to sleep on thin mattresses on the floor because we needed a cooker more than beds. Over the next few months we collected some very eccentric pieces of furniture like wicker chairs and tables that got eaten by termites in six months, rickety bookshelves for our many books, and a large kitchen table that sags in the middle and that we have to this day.

The house was progressing nicely, and finally it felt a bit like home. However, some things still felt very strange. We had to dump our rubbish in the nearby rubbish tip, and every time we did so the same three children would come run-

ning out of their huts. They would tear open the plastic rubbish bags and search for food and anything they could play with. This made me feel very ashamed as we were throwing away things that were important to them. After that, we always cleaned the plastic water containers that they were rummaging around for, and gave them food. It was something, but I still felt bad.

We were learning something new every day and this was hard for Emily who was trying to concentrate on her A-levels, which she was doing by correspondence. Although she was extremely committed to her work, there were so many interesting African things happening all the time and she felt she couldn't miss them. Some friends and family had tried to persuade her to stay in England and work on her A-levels there, but she stuck to her guns and left with us to start a new life. I was so happy she came as I needed a sister along with my three brothers to go through this huge change with me. It was good for Emily to come and have a taste of our new life and it was great for my mother. Mum and Emily are very close and they help each other with their problems, they also make each other laugh and whenever there was a huge problem, they would solve it by cracking up.

In England Mum was never fond of having pets in the house because she felt it was cruel to enclose them. But within weeks of arriving at Thuso we were given two puppies that Emily loved to distraction. Their mother had been poisoned and the puppies were not weaned, so Emily had to get up countless times in the night to feed them. She and Mum would sit up for hours chatting and giggling with the new members of our family. In Africa everyone has dogs because they are good protection for your property and they kill snakes. Everything was free and open at Thuso, and Mum was happy to have dogs since she didn't feel that they were trapped.

However, rabies was a slight anxiety. This was the first time I had ever heard about this virus and we were warned not to go near strange dogs as they might be carrying it. Rabies is transmitted by bite and unless you are treated quite quickly you can die. The virus gets into the brain and makes dogs extremely aggressive and want to bite everyone they see. Rabies is a serious problem in Botswana and the government is trying to do something about it. At first we were puzzled by all the dogs we saw with red paint sprayed on their foreheads. It turned out that these were the dogs that had been inoculated for rabies by government vets. The ones without paint got shot on sight, so everyone made sure their dogs were vaccinated.

One day, when I was seven, we were driving to school when a dog ran across the road, reminding me of a conversation Mum and Emily had had about rabies. 'What's a rabbit dog, Mum?' I asked. They burst out laughing and I didn't know what all the fuss was about. They haven't let me live it down to this day and one of the puppies was immediately named Rabbit. Sadly Rabbit died a year later of parvo, another dangerous virus, and we were heartbroken.

The Thuso house was never quite right, and no matter how hard we tried, it didn't feel like home. After a while, thick, black muck started coming out of the taps, and the water smelled terrible. We had to tie cloths around the taps to filter the water, and had to change the cloths regularly as the taps got blocked with black slime. We called people in who told us everything was fine: it was 'just Africa'. But it all started to get a little bit too disgusting, so we decided to get a sample of the water tested. We were told it was dirty because the holding tank was extremely old and needed to be changed. We couldn't possibly afford a new tank, so Mum decided to clean the old one. This involved a lot of ladders, scraping and Mum nearly breaking her neck several times, but it made no difference at all to the colour and rich smell of the water. Well, lovely, we thought, this is Africa! But after a few months we could not put up with it any more, so we decided to move house.

THE MISSION HOUSE

TRAVERS

WE MOVED INTO a huge, beautiful, white house called the Mission House (its name was slightly ironic as you will find out). It was a fifteen-minute drive from town in the opposite direction from Thuso. Everyone loved this spectacular house dearly, and it was here that we started to feel more at home in Maun.

The Mission House was also perfect for our crazy family and the plethora of dogs we had acquired over a very short time. The water was a slightly paler shade of brown, marginally less smelly than Thuso's, and, happily, without black muck and slime. Our recently made friends, the Longdens, helped us move our very few belongings into the Mission House. Tim and Bryony, who became Mum's dearest friends, ran an ostrich farm that produced ostrich meat and skin. They happily lugged our stuff over in their ancient Bedford truck. It only took one trip and when we unloaded everything, the house still looked empty. We never really managed to fill the rooms, but the open floors provided us with the best space imaginable to learn how to roller blade.

Oakley with an orphaned baby cheetah at the Longden's farm.

One of Maun's many surprises was the roller-blading rink, which became the centre of our social life. It took us ages to find it the first time, weaving our way along a maze of sandy tracks and getting hopelessly lost. The rink was built by an eccentric, generous-hearted American carpenter called Sandy Greer, who opens it to the whole community six nights a week. Anyone can turn up and learn to play roller hockey. Sandy's rules are simple and clear, play fair and look out for each other. He is a very laid-back man but we have all learned that he has eyes in the back of his head and never misses an injustice. It was there that we made our friends and learned a lot about our new life. Among many other things, we

learned that in Maun age doesn't matter. Children of all ages play together without embarrassment, and mix very easily with the adults. We made our first tottering attempts on the rink within weeks of moving in and Mum cleverly realised that our elastic money had to be stretched to pay for roller blades of our own. We practised every second of the day and did our initial falling and crashing on the veranda of the Mission House. We put our skates on first thing in the morning and for the next few weeks lived our life on wheels. We set the table on skates, went to the loo on skates, cooked on skates, and even did school wearing our blades. Within a few weeks we could play hockey with the other kids (though not very well) and soon after that we were playing with the adults. Nothing but rain closed the rink.

Our new life was spent almost entirely outdoors. The Mission House's garden had some beautiful trees. There were massive strangler figs, which we used to climb for hours, swinging on the long vines that hung down to the ground. There was also a magnificent tree called an African mangosteen, which produced the most succulent fruits you can imagine, tasting like a cross between a lemon and a mango. We spent days in this tree picking and eating the fruits until our stomachs hurt. We also had a lovely view of the Thamalakane River. The river is wide, full of lilies and aquatic plant life, and is home to crocodiles and hippos. One hippo would sometimes pay us a visit and would graze at the bottom of our garden in the cool of the night; very different from the hedgehog that used to come into our garden at night in Hollybush. The Thamalakane River dries up some years but is replenished by rainfall and seasonal floods from the Okavango Delta.

Within days of moving in, people arrived asking for jobs, because in Botswana a new person in the community means a new job. The first to call was a young man named Johnny, who wanted to help in our garden. Johnny was not only a gardener but also a teacher to us all. He taught us which snakes were harmful (like the deadly Boomslang that slithered into Angus's bedroom one day while he was reading a book), how to avoid being stung by scorpions lurking in the woodpile and why the river was so dangerous, and he gave us lots of other confusing information about the new place that had become our home. Oddly, he was terrified of chameleons, which we knew were harmless. He swore that Oakley would die laughing if one bit him. Mum wryly muttered 'what a way to go', but Johnny was clearly very upset. We later discovered that chameleons are bad medicine in Johnny's culture.

During this time we also started home schooling. Our mother was, and still is, our teacher. When we started school Oakley was, at two, still too young to join us and was bored when we worked. Johnny noticed this and would take Oakley on long walks in the garden and along the river-bed where Oakley would try to catch grasshoppers and birds and learn about how they worked. We felt very safe when Oaks was with him, as we knew he would protect him against all mishaps. Johnny became a very important member of our expanding family.

Our next-door neighbours, the Sandenbergs, helped us through many difficult times. Their kids are called Jethro, Baz and Zora. Jethro took us under his wing when we first arrived and took very good care of us. Mum really listened to his advice even though he was only nine. Baz was and still is a wild child

and we were astonished to see him riding on the bull-bar or hanging off the car's roof as his mum sped along the sandy roads. In England everyone has to be strapped in, and long journeys are not much fun, but, as Baz showed us, there is a lot more freedom to be had in Africa. Baz has one of the kindest faces I know and has grown up to be a very deep thinker. Zora was only four, and came over a lot to play with Oaks. Her favourite game was dressing him up in her clothes, and Oaks, who loved her dearly, would willingly dap about wearing pink sparkly shoes and Little Mermaid headgear. Baz and Jethro would rather have died than let their little sister dress them up. Oakley used to play with Baz a lot too and together they were a very naughty little team. They used to climb across our fence and run to Anne Sandenberg's house. If Anne was not there they slithered through the cat flap and made a beeline for the overflowing jar of sweets by her telephone. Anne Sandenberg is the granny and her house is always full of children; we are always welcome there. Anne is a brave, pioneering woman who arrived in Maun over forty years ago. In those days Maun was virtually cut off during the rainy season, and she would have to queue for a day for fresh vegetables to feed her three children. Anne founded Women Against Rape in the early

1990s, and over the years this organisation has helped and protected many needy women and children in and around Maun. Soon after we arrived, Mum volunteered to work with Anne, and stayed with the organisation for nearly two years.

Despite all the information and good advice we were given in those early days, we of course made mistakes. One of my friends wanted Angus and me to swim across the river to collect a boat on the bank opposite our house. We had been told never to do this because of the crocodiles and hippos. When the crocs weren't basking they lurked in among the lilies waiting to prey on whatever animal came down to drink. Despite all this, crossing the river seemed a fun idea and we were easily persuaded. Halfway across I got tangled among the lily stems. I called to my friend to help me but she did not hear and carried on swimming. I panicked and started to shout very loudly but unfortunately this drew the attention of the next-door neighbours and Mum. The neighbours screamed at us to get out, Mum simply called to us – when she is really angry she is quite terrifyingly quiet. She was sure that I was going to be attacked by a crocodile, which turned out to be a very reasonable anxiety, for in the last five years we know of several people who have been killed this way. I finally managed to free myself, and swam across to the safety of the boat. When we got back to the other side everyone was angry except Mum who was still shocked and quiet. We were punished severely, and never swam in the river again, not because of our punishment, but because we saw how scared Mum was.

Seven months had passed since we had moved from England, and it was now our first Christmas in Africa. Life in the Mission House was a wonderful and busy time for all of us; everything was new and even Christmas was about to be reinvented. I was the happiest I had been for a long time but there was a gap in all our hearts that needed to be filled. We were missing Dad terribly but our cloud of sadness soon passed when we were told that he was coming for Christmas. I will leave it to Maisie to tell you about our first African Christmas as it meant a great deal to her.

"We were used to Dad being away for long periods of time because he is an actor, but we had never been parted for this long before.

When the big day came we all jumbled into our very rusty old Toyota and sped to the airport to pick him up. Finally Dad stepped out of the plane on to the tarmac. We watched him take his first breath of African air. We were calling and calling as hard as we could but he did not hear us through the thick glass. Then he looked up and spotted us. We all ran down the steps and flung our arms around him.

The flights to Africa from America are so expensive that sometimes we don't see him for years. (Once, when money was tight, Travers kindly let me take his place and I flew to see Dad in England. We can cope with missing him now because we are used to it, but it is still hard.)

When we saw he had two massive suitcases we knew they would be full of presents. On the way back home Oakley kept peeking in the back, seeking them out. We told Dad about our life in Africa and all the extraordinary things that had happened to us.

Dad at the Sandenberg's

We showed him to his room in the Mission House. There were spiders everywhere, and poor Dad was freaked but the boys reassured him. Spiders are in fact very useful as they eat the mosquitoes and other bugs you don't want hanging around. 'Wait a moment, that one *is* very poisonous.' cried Angus, as he

noticed a violin spider crawling across the ceiling. Dad leaped back looking very anxious. Angus was exaggerating; violin spiders are poisonous and can give quite nasty bites, but only if you leave the bites unattended, we get them all the time and they're not too bad. Dad wasn't that grateful to Gus as the spider came to rest in a corner near his bed. Gus killed it for him and Dad was very proud of him. That night we had a candle-lit dinner on the veranda. We caught up on seven months of news and sat listening to the grunting of the hippos in the river. We all slept like logs but Dad was up all night killing every spider he laid eyes on, poor soul.

During the week we showed him around the town and surrounding villages. We introduced him to our friends and took him out into the bush. We also took him shopping. While all the decorations were up and the shops full of mince pies and chocolates, something was wrong. This was our first African Christmas and to me it just didn't feel like Christmas. It was hot and we didn't have a real tree, only an acacia branch sprayed with silver paint and hung with decorations. We couldn't hang our stockings over a fireplace – instead we had to hang them on the veranda and hope it didn't rain in the night. I remembered Hollybush Christmases with roaring fires and the smell of the pine tree. Even after five years in Africa, Christmas never feels quite right here. But Oakley, who was only two, had none of these memories and could hardly wait for the day to come. In fact he could barely breathe he was so excited.

On Christmas Eve the stockings went up and Oakley put out whisky and mince pies for Father Christmas, and left carrots for the reindeers. As night fell we made a fire in the garden and sat around it with little pieces of paper in our hands. They were letters and we had written on them what we wanted from Father Christmas. We all read them out loud before putting them in the fire. The paper burns and the letters fly up for the fairies to collect. Then Mum read us 'Bill Frog to the Rescue'. She has had this book since she was eight and it is now very battered and torn, but we all love it dearly and she reads it every Christmas Eve. She brought it out when we moved to Africa, with many, many other books. (In fact when we arrived we only had six suitcases for clothes and things, but twenty packing cases of books!)

At six the next morning we woke Mum because, according to tradition, we all have to open stockings together; she tottered in hardly awake and joined us on Dad's bed. We ripped things open and threw paper all around but of course Travers, being Travers, did everything slowly. This was torture for the rest of us because when we had all finished, his stocking was still half full. After Christmas breakfast Oakley, who was smeared with chocolate and having a sugar rush, kept asking Mum and Dad when we were going to have our presents from them. He

was very disappointed when Mum said that he was going to have to wait. Five years down the line Oaks still has problems with the 'w' word.

We all played with the things we had in our stockings and at eleven we were called into the sitting room and each of us was handed clues. Mum is very good at treasure hunts and makes up really good clues with riddles in them. The clues led us all over the house and garden and finally to the car; they led us into and around town until we ended up at an office where Mum sometimes worked. Dad told us to shut our eyes… 'Open them!' he cried a minute later and we couldn't believe what we saw. There were three huge bikes and a little black scooter for Oakley. Emily got a Leatherman knife that she was very proud of, and used a lot on her travels around the world that she started a few months later.

Baz, Zora and Jethro also had bikes, so now we could all ride around together while our parents talked. Christmas lunch with the Sandenbergs was spread out in the garden. Dad got on well with our friends and they thought he was very funny. We stayed until eleven at night and then rode home to bed on our bikes. Mum always leaves a small surprise present under our pillow and Oaks, who was not expecting that, thought it was magic.

It was wonderful spending our first African Christmas together as a family.

We have had Christmas in many different places: one deep in the Okavango Delta, where we watched the sun set on Christmas Eve from a wooded dugout canoe surrounded by waterlilies. That Boxing Day we took a walk and watched a pride of lions eating a warthog. Our stockings have been hung up in trees, at the end of our beds, and lately in our mess tent. They are always filled with familiar things and I love Christmas wherever we are. ''

Just after our first African Christmas something awful happened. It was my twelfth birthday and Mum had organised a surprise birthday dinner. While we were out celebrating, our house was robbed. The thieves took almost everything we had, which was not much, but it included all the Christmas presents as well as some of my birthday gifts. Everybody tried not to mind because the people here don't own a lot and live on very little. But it was not right that they stole from us. What hurt us most was that the thieves turned out to be Johnny and his brother. We had to do a horrible thing and fire our wonderful Johnny. This was the first of many firings as our trusting mother continuously forgave and reinstated him shortly after he was dismissed.

After a year in Maun Emily had to go back to England to work in order to earn money for a trip around the world. This was shockingly sad. Ems is six years older than me and was always there, laughing, bossing and cuddling; though we were all very proud of her, none of us had really imagined what life would be like without her. Originally, Emily was planning to travel with her friend Sarah, but as Sarah had a baby, she decided not to go and Emily chose to travel the world by herself. Emily's courage was inspirational but we all worried about her a lot. She left us while we were still in the Mission House and it still feels strange that she has missed so much of our life out here. I felt nervous because now I was the oldest and the one left to look after everyone when Mum was away. Poor Maisie was at the mercy of three brothers and missed the girly times she had had with her big sister. I think to this day Mum still aches with the missing of Emily.

A week after Emily left, Angus and I got very sick and tested positive for malaria. We had a nasty few weeks lying in bed with a high fever and throwing up; it was a disgusting thing to go through. To get rid of the malaria, we had to take some really horrible drugs, which made us feel worse. Luckily we didn't have to go to the hospital and we both pulled through okay. We had a brilliant doctor called Patrick Akhiwu, from Nigeria, who didn't just help both Angus and me but also looked after our worried and anxious mum. He reassured her that both of us would be fine and showed her how she could look after us. We all grew to love Patrick. He was, and still is, very patient. I think he found us a sur-

THE BILHARZIA CYCLE

An infected person urinates in a river

mouth

ventral Sucker

female

Ventral groove

male

Snail, Real Size

The blood fluke, male and female during pairing.

the urine contains fluke eggs

the eggs hatch

the immature flukes enter snails.

the now larger, (but still young) flukes enter into a person, swimming in a river, through skin.

prising family. He always made time to comfort Mum and to help us feel that we could cope with anything. Oakley loves him because he keeps sweets in his surgery and will dig in his pockets and bring out tiny plastic helicopters or aeroplanes. Patrick calls Oaks Huckleberry Finn.

The next person to get sick in the family was me – again. This time it was bilharzia, which I had picked up by swimming in the river! Bilharzia is caused by a water-borne parasite that has a water snail as its intermediate host. After it leaves the snail, the parasite swims through the water and penetrates the skin of a human. It may also be taken in with the drinking water. Once inside the body it lives in blood vessels in the intestines or urinary system causing symptoms such as headaches, diarrhoea, vomiting, anaemia and stomach cramps. I was very sick for three months, and had to go to Patrick Akhiwu every other day.

Poor Patrick scratched his head as my symptoms were very confusing, and none of the blood tests gave a clue as to what was wrong. I was throwing up and had a very painful stomach, I had bad headaches but no fever, and I generally felt rotten. One night I got horribly sick, worse than ever, and still nobody knew what was wrong with me. Mum ran to the only person who had a telephone and asked for help.

They called Allison, a remarkable Scottish nurse who deals with emergency medical evacuations. Allison reassured us but decided I must leave straight away, as it was possible I had appendicitis. She put a drip in me, and then called Johannesburg to arrange for a medical jet to be sent up to collect me. While all of this was going on around me I felt very nervous and daunted by the journey that lay ahead, but also in an odd way excited. Allison had to wake up the Maun airport staff so they could be ready to receive the jet from South Africa. The jet arrived with a doctor and a nurse on board. They gave me a sedative, and the next thing I knew I was in a strange bed with needles in my arms, still feeling terrible. It took doctors in the hospital ten days and many blood tests to find out it was bilharzia. The treatment was simple: I took just a few pills, and in two days I was feeling a bit better. Mum was very relieved. She was so worried over those weeks and lost a lot of sleep, but she regained her colour and was very pleased when we finally boarded the Air Botswana plane and flew home to Maun. We were greeted with many hugs. Our next-door neighbours the Sandenbergs had looked after the rest of the family beautifully.

Sadly the rent on the Mission House went up and we could not afford to live there any longer. We had to leave our white house and move into a new stage of our African adventure.

THE CROCODILE FARM HOUSE

ANGUS

AFTER MANY WEEKS of searching, we found another, much cheaper house. It was a change from the Mission House as it was situated on a crocodile farm, fourteen kilometres out of Maun. The area was rich in wildlife and we often saw spotted hyenas, genets, jackals and sometimes a cape fox, which is quite rare. The hundreds of crocs that lived on the farm were kept in big pens behind our house. Even though our new living space was small, just one room and a shower, it was beautiful. It had a thatched roof held up by wooden poles and reed walls. The thatch made it cool in summer but it was freezing in winter because the wind howled through the reed walls and blew clouds of dust down from the ancient thatch. The house wasn't exactly luxurious. The showerhead was so clogged with dirt that no amount of scrubbing would clean it, so we took it off and stood under the trickle produced by the pipe. In the end we preferred to bathe in a large zinc tub. In spite of this, the house had a lot of character and we grew to enjoy its eccentricities.

A generator with a mind of its own provided electricity for the farm. Although it was supposed to run from 7 a.m. to 11 p.m., it seemed to switch itself off at will and regularly plunged us into darkness. It never ran the hot water, as we didn't have an electric boiler. To get hot water we had to put a fire under the 'chip boiler', a modified gas cylinder with a chimney. The water, contained in the gas cylinder, was heated by the fire and then carried to the house by a plastic pipe that was prone to burst at any time, usually when I had just soaped up. Oakley loved collecting wood for the boiler and we quickly got used to running this system. The kitchen was tiny and the pipes to the sink were continuously leaking, forming an assemblage of puddles on the floor. The electrical wires weren't earthed either, so if you plugged anything in while you were in the kitchen, you stood a very good chance of being

electrocuted. The fridge handle was metal so you would sometimes receive a shock when opening it. We all claim responsibility for a simple act of pure genius; we wrapped a dishcloth round the handle and our shocking days were over.

Our giant bed made of a mass of single and double beds crammed together took up one end of the house. This was very cosy and we named it our *Frankie Furbo* bed, for we all slept in it like William Wharton's fox family. We would read stories and go to sleep to the sound of bullfrogs in the rainy season. As the night drew on, the bed gradually filled up, Mum would stay up writing or working by candlelight, until she eventually squeezed in amongst us and fell asleep.

We made the outside of the house very comfortable and lived mostly outdoors. We had our dining table and chairs set up in the garden, along with our eclectic array of sofas (which migrated inside the house in the winter, where it was at least a degree warmer). When we first came to the croc farm, the garden was non-existent, but soon Mum planted many flowers, herbs and vegetables and our garden flour-

LEFT We often heard spotted Hyenas calling at night at the croc farm.

BELOW Oakley loved collecting wood for the 'chip boiler'

ished. It did this somewhat strangely, however, as Oakley showed a deep interest in sprinkling seeds everywhere and poking them into every nook and cranny. Our greatest challenge in the garden was the resident Black Mamba. By now we had grown used to having snakes in our lives but we were, and still are, sensibly wary of the highly poisonous mambas. We resolved the problem by pouring petrol around its hideout in the flowerpots. Snakes hate the fumes given off by the petrol, and it also irritates their skin when they slither over it. Typically, Mum, who knows nothing of half measures, poured petrol all around the house 'just to be sure'. We never saw the mamba again; and didn't light a match for a while.

Once again we had many people coming to the house and asking us for a job, and this is how Inspector came into our lives. Inspector was a fascinating man. In his time he had travelled around the Okavango Delta putting up Tsetse fly traps for the government. He had also been a baker and assured us he was an expert gardener. He spoke English very well and adored Oakley, who in turn worshipped him and followed him around like a puppy. I remember Inspector interrupting school one morning by bursting into the house with tears pouring down his face. We were relieved to find they were tears of laughter and trooped out to see what he was laughing at. We discovered that Oakley had locked himself in the car. He had wound up the windows, and he was sitting in among the pedals with a dog biscuit in one hand and a can of beer in the other. 'Oakley,' we shouted, knocking on the window. He beamed up at us and after unlocking the door, he trotted out, still clutching his beer. Mum was relieved to find that only half the beer had been consumed and that it was a low alcohol brand. As for the dog biscuits they were anti-tartar and probably good for his teeth!

Inspector shared Oakley's interest in alcohol and took great pleasure in deplet

ing my Mum's supply. He often came to work bleary-eyed and walking seemed to require a lot of concentration. Mum fired him many times, but, like Johnny, he never remained unemployed for more than a day or two, as he always came back full of remorse. He provided Oakley with a stream of unlikely treasures, and rose to his greatest height when he turned up, very early one morning, bearing a bright orange cockerel in his arms. Oakley's new pet put an end to the few scraps of sleep we managed to snatch at night, as between the dogs barking, the frogs croaking and the cockerel calling there was never a moment's silence.

Oakley's fascination with the car did not end with the dog biscuit incident. One day we were all in the kitchen cooking lunch when we heard a loud cry coming from the driveway. We charged out and to our horror saw the car halfway down the drive, wedged into a bush, with Oakley's little face peeking out the window. He looked racked with anxiety and fear: 'Will mummy be cwoss with me?' Mummy wasn't cross at all, but ran to the car, half crying, half laughing, and swept Oaks into her arms.

'I'm sowwy, I'm sowwy,' he whimpered. Mum peered into the car and saw that Oakley had accidentally let off the hand brake, causing the car to roll down the sloping driveway. He was lucky that the wheels had been slightly turned and the vehicle had veered off into a nearby bush, otherwise he would have crashed right through the flimsy reed wall that protected the crocodile pen at the end of our drive. From then on we parked the car well away from the road that led to the pens and tried to get into the habit of locking it, though Mum is phobic in her hatred of keys. Inspector, out of his love for Oaks, kept an eye on the boy and the car.

The croc pens were cause for concern. Crocodiles would frequently burst out and roam the roads of the farm, dragging their colossal bulk around on their short stumpy legs, their cold eyes locked straight ahead and their dagger teeth protruding out of their deceptively smiling mouths. Even though they aren't as lethal on land as they are in water, crocodiles can still break a man's leg with their tail or inflict a deadly bite. We had all seen the agility of these beasts when we once threw a dead Spitting Cobra into a pen. With the speed of light they leaped up and fought over the fast-disappearing snake carcass. Travers and I had also visited the baby croc pens, and saw that the youngsters were as fast as the adults. We had to be very careful when we picked them up, for they could whip out of your hands as quick as lightning.

Crocs were not such a threat in the winter when they are not so aggressive and do not want to eat big meals. The enzymes in their stomachs become inactive in the colder months, therefore if they were to eat a large amount of food it would just rot in their stomachs and they would eventually die. We still had to be careful, though, for an angry croc may still lash out. One of the main problems with croc bites is infection; people have died after an attack not because of the wounds or even loss of blood but because they weren't put on a major course of antibiotics. We were not allowed to walk around the farm without each other for company and Oaks was not allowed to walk around at all without an adult. Some of the animals that escaped were massive, and a man named Zambo had the unenviable job of recapturing them. When someone located a hole in the fence they would report it to Zambo, who would go with a truckload of men to find the fugitive croc. Once the croc was found the men would make a loop in a rope and

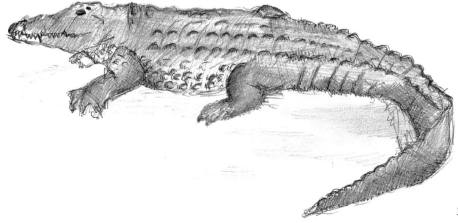

slip it round the animal's chest, then they would tie the rope to the car and drag the croc slowly back to its pen. This requires a huge amount of skill and courage, for the crocodile is always fighting and has lethal weapons at both ends of its body. We would watch the whole process in fascination and follow behind the crocodile at a safe distance, holding Oakley back as he always wanted to lend a hand. Tragically, Zambo was killed by these very crocodiles a few years later. He tried to clear a drain in the croc pens and was attacked. Mum and Oakley had visited him a few days before and he was his usual beaming self.

Zambo and his family lived in a village on the farm along with the other farm workers. They formed a close-knit community and lived in mud and reed huts that they had built themselves. Many of the elderly women on the farm wove baskets to sell to tourists that passed by, and they were left in charge of the children while their parents went to work. Often the younger kids would come over to our house and play with Oakley, and Travers and I played soccer with the older ones every evening at the campsite. The people on the farm were very poor and the village was quite far from town. This meant that in the event of illness or an accident the hospital was inaccessible. Our mother soon became known as Ma Doctor.

One morning, soon after we had settled into our new house, a woman arrived at the door asking for help. She was very distressed, as she had been stung by a bee, and the right side of her face had swollen up to twice its normal size. Mum gave her a homeopathic remedy and she was better in a day. This seemed like magic and from then on people with all kinds of injuries started flooding in. Some were not serious; men came staggering in with bloodshot eyes, complaining that their head hurt. Mum would ask if they had been drinking the night before and when they confessed she would send them away with some Alka Seltzer. However, some wounds were very nasty. A boy that Travers and I had been playing football with came to Mum with a hugely swollen foot. To our horror it was one and a half times bigger than his other foot. He said he had been chasing chickens and had been skewered by a branch. Some of the branch must have broken off inside his foot, which was now turning green. The poor boy was in great pain; Mum, though she found it hard to hurt him, had to use an Aspivenin reverse-syringe to suck out the poison to remove the source of infection, and the boy bravely held back his screams. She dressed his foot in a porridge poultice as this draws out poison very effectively. He came to us every day for a week to have his dressing changed and fresh porridge applied; after seven days the wound had healed. The people on the farm loved my mother but soon found out she couldn't cure every sickness.

One evening a woman who lived on the farm came to us with terrible abdominal pain. She was pregnant and her boyfriend had punched her in the stomach. Domestic violence and sexual abuse is a serious problem in Botswana. We learned about this through Mum's voluntary work for Women Against Rape. The pregnant woman had serious bruising on her stomach and Mum immediately drove her to the hospital in town. Tragically she lost the baby a few days later. The man who beat her was put in prison for only three days and warned not to do it again, which made us all feel very angry.

A few weeks later the same woman asked us to visit her mother who had a bad foot. She took us to a small settlement a couple of kilometres off the road to Maun. Rubbish was strewn everywhere and the mud walls of her mother's hut were collapsing. As we drove up we saw her three grandchildren peeking out of her house and goats eating plastic bags in the yard. We were heartbroken to see that the old woman had no fingers or toes as they had been eaten away by leprosy. She tottered towards us, with a big smile, balancing a bowl between her fingerless hands. She looked after her grandchildren by herself, and she did the washing, cooking and cleaning by hand with no help. My mother got out of the car and greeted the remarkable woman, with the customary greeting 'Dumela Ma'.

The old woman's foot had a gaping hole in it. My mother asked for some water to clean it and one of the children who had been watching us from behind a tree ran to fetch it. Meanwhile, Mum put on some surgical gloves and started to dig out the impacted sand from the wound. The old lady showed no sign of pain and kept on chatting to her daughter. Leprosy eats away at nerve endings and so all sensitivity is lost; this is why so many wounds are left unattended and become infected. Once the wound was cleansed we could see how deep it was – Mum could fit most of her hand inside. We dressed it but felt that Dr Patrick should see the wound and advise us how to help the woman. The old grandmother was very excited about a trip to town, even though it was only to see the doctor, and wore her best dress. When Patrick inspected her foot he told us it was the bacterial form of leprosy, which is only contagious by close contact over time. When this disease is diagnosed early it is easily healed, but sadly this woman had probably been hidden away by her family, as strange sicknesses and deformities often embarrass people in Botswana. Indeed, in South Africa lepers and convicts were sent to live in isolation on Robben Island, where Nelson Mandela was incarcerated. Patrick told us that we should encourage her to wear shoes at all times and clean the wound out regularly until it was healed. We saw her often after this and always received the same warm, smiling greeting. Unfortunately, when we moved from the croc farm, we lost touch with this courageous woman. Two years later we met her again by chance. She and her daughter, who now had a new baby, had moved to a village closer to town and looked very well and happy. We were delighted to see she was still wearing shoes.

While Mum was very popular as Ma Doctor with the farm workers, our family was a source of profound irritation to other people who lived on the farm. We are appallingly noisy and our dogs barked all night. Over the months we had accumulated many dogs; the two females we had acquired at the Mission House turned out to be excellent breeders. Sadly one of them died of canine parvovirus, a virulent disease. The other bitch was called Boro, and she produced a litter of eleven pups. We gave some away but kept three and we named them Simba, Beetle and Crumple. They came with us to the croc farm along with Boro. Later Boro had yet another litter of eleven puppies and we kept yet one more, Smudge. At this point there was near rebellion; no one on the farm would speak to us because our 'pack' caused so much noise. Boro was an excellent dog and well house trained, unlike her children. She had survived parvo and had been badly beaten and then abandoned before she came to us. She was a very loving dog but fierce in battle. We were heartbroken when we learned that two huge dogs had attacked and killed her while we were away in the bush.

The other animals that featured in our life on the croc farm were rats. The infestation hit us when the rainy season came. They were all over the place: in the cupboards, under the beds, in the thatch, on the table. They pooped and peed everywhere, and it was not unusual to have one crawl over your head at night. Don't be too disgusted, these were not huge sewer rats but much smaller and prettier acacia rats. Nevertheless, it was not much fun. We laid out rat poison but soon learned that this method of extermination had its drawbacks. They died in the most inaccessible places and we could find them only by following the stench of decomposing flesh. Once located, the rat then had to be removed; we found long fondue sticks to be the perfect tool. I had the unenviable task of digging them out while Mum burned joss sticks to clear the air. As poisoning was not a great success, we turned to traps. I kept a booklet and wrote down the number and size of all the rats we caught. Our record was twelve in one night, and the largest was twenty-eight centimetres from tail to nose but on average they measured twelve centimetres.

Donkeys were a problem too. In Botswana they are used to carry things around and to haul an extraordinary array of carts. These are made out of any old bits and pieces of wood or tyre that can be nailed together. Some of the carts are painted with bright colours and even have umbrellas to keep the driver in the shade. The donkeys would roam free and our garden was heaven to them. They regularly chewed the tops of lovingly nursed plants and vegetables. Gardening in a desert environment is no mean feat, and we had to squeeze what we could from the remnant bath water (pitch-black after Oakley had bathed in it) and collect water from the leaky pipes to sprinkle the plants. But it was actually

Inspector who caused the death of most of our plants. His weeding was creative and arbitrary, but my favourite image is of him standing in the doorway with his arms full of spinach. He had been asked to pick some leaves for lunch. 'I have done it,' he said proudly. In fact, what he had done was to root up all the plants that were meant to last us for the summer. Mum found it very funny, and we had a huge spinach salad for lunch.

The year we spent on the croc farm was the year of the red-billed quelea. These are tiny little birds that came to the farm in their millions to roost. They drank from the croc pens or from the muddy pans that had formed in the river-bed after the rains. They would all swoop down together and this caused many of them to get stuck in the mud. Maisie would regularly arrive in the house clutching a cardboard box full of minute birds she had rescued. While they were roosting near our house the ground literally was inches deep in their poop and the smell of ammonia was overpowering. Nevertheless it was breathtaking watching them fly in tight formation. At night we would go to sleep listening to them chirruping in the trees, or lulled by the reverberation of their wings as they took off in synchrony, sounding like a great ocean.

By the end of our first two years in Africa we had overcome many fears, developed new skills and had settled happily into our new life. However we had no idea that our greatest challenge was yet to come. While we were making homes and learning to stand on our own two feet, we were also exploring a whole new dimension, the African bush. This was to change our lives forever.

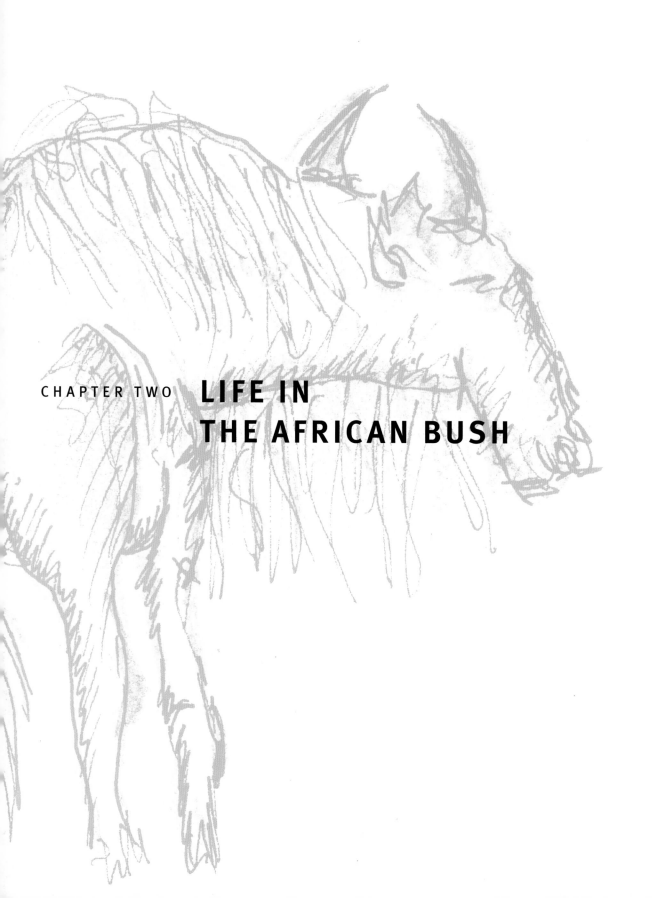

CHAPTER TWO **LIFE IN
THE AFRICAN BUSH**

OUR FIRST EXPERIENCES
OF THE BUSH
TRAVERS

WHEN WE FIRST MOVED to Maun we often drove into the bush just for the day. We first started these trips when we were staying in the Mission House. People in town thought we were insane, as 'going to the bush' to them seemed such a mission. Most people would take huge amounts of equipment with them and go for days. Not us – after school we would just pull a picnic together, hurl things into a cooler box, load blankets, books, cool drinks and Oakley's latest treasures into our Toyota. The car had open safari seats on the back, which were refreshing in the hot and dry seasons but miserable in the wetter months. Mum and Emily would sit in the front and the rest of us piled in the back with the wind on our faces.

Getting to the bush took about two hours: forty-five minutes on a tar road that had just been built, and then half an hour on a corrugated road which would throw us about in the car until our heads rattled. We were always relieved to see the water pump by the side of the road, for it was here that we turned off on to the sand track that would take us to the buffalo fence. This fence is guarded by a man who lives in a metal hut; he has no shower, just a tub, he cooks on a small fire and has one dog to keep him company. This lonely man's job is to open and close the gate and do a daily patrol of the fence. The buffalo fence is there to separate domestic cattle from wildlife and thereby prevent the transmission of diseases. Sometimes wild animals like giraffes get caught in the wires. But the good thing about the fence is that it prevents domestic animals from moving on to land that has been set aside for wildlife. For us it was always exciting to go through it, because from that

moment, anything could be around the next corner: elephants, buffaloes or some new animals we had not yet seen. It was always a beautiful game drive, and in those days it seemed beyond our wildest dreams that this very trip would one day become the journey home.

Running in the Okavango.

In the beginning we would often drive around and see nothing. But after several trips our eyes sharpened and we started to become more aware of our new surroundings. We would often see animals that were unknown to us like wildebeests and warthogs. Wildebeests are hideously ugly antelopes (Mum would kill me for saying that because she loves them); you might know them as gnus. They have got scrawny legs, large upper bodies, hairy necks and their skin is a dull blue/grey. Warthogs are my Dad's favourite animal. They look like wild boars but have larger tusks, they trot busily with their tails pointing up into the sky and look as if they have just forgotten something. When we saw animals unknown to us we would plough through the many guidebooks that Mum had bought us to try to identify them. We would drive for hours around the sand tracks exploring and stopping to have our picnics while watching zebras grazing, or just looking at the shapes of the trees against the skyline. Everything was so different to the landscape we had left behind – instead of rolling hills and bluebell woods, we now had flat, tawny savannah and shady acacia forests.

During these trips Angus and I started to learn about the birds, and watch for

ABOVE Warthog, Dad's favourite animal.

vultures in the sky. Descending vultures often mean that there is a carcass around, and if we were lucky, we might catch a glimpse of a predator, like a lion, leopard, hyena, cheetah or even a little jackal. Maisie's eyes never ceased to amaze us, as she could, seemingly without trying, spot a leopard hiding deep inside a bush. To this day no one in the family has developed Maisie's eye for tiny hidden things. Aged two, Oakley was not learning the names of everyday farm animals, but of wild animals that were living free. As he got a bit older he loved to join in a car game that Mum used to teach us the animals' scientific names. Oakley learned that the elephant's scientific name is *Loxodonta africana* and that a giraffe's is *Giraffa camelopardalis*. As night started to fall we would reluctantly head back to Maun to make supper and fall into bed.

BELOW Burchell's Zebra.

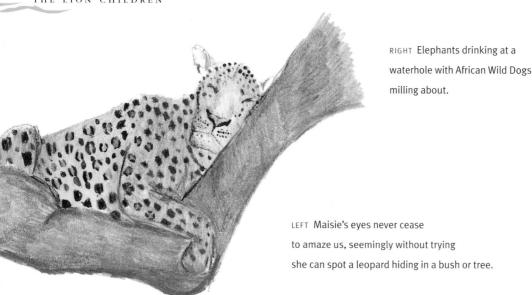

RIGHT Elephants drinking at a
waterhole with African Wild Dogs
milling about.

LEFT Maisie's eyes never cease
to amaze us, seemingly without trying
she can spot a leopard hiding in a bush or tree.

We had our fair share of adventures in the bush: getting stuck, getting punctures, getting lost and coping with charging elephants. On one trip we had to tackle some particularly difficult challenges. We had packed the car and were heading out of town when there was a noise under the bonnet. This was not unusual as the truck broke down almost daily. We stopped and tried to find out what was causing the hideous clanking sound. This time the fan belt had snapped. I did not know anything about cars in those days: I still thought if you had a problem you took it to a garage and I did not think you could fix things yourself. I was absolutely clueless. I am now quite well informed about cars and can change a fan belt with no problem. Anyway, on that day everyone thought, 'there goes our bush trip', but Mum told us not to worry as we could work something out. As usual it was the Longdens who saved us; we had broken down near their house and they thought nothing of lending us a car for the day.

It was excellent to drive in a smart car for a change. We went to our secret picnic tree (it looked exactly the same as the fig tree that was at the Mission House), and as usual Mum first scouted the area for snakes or dangerous animals, then unloaded us and unpacked the food. We ate while watching a breeding herd of elephants walk towards the water hole in front of us. They drank slowly and then headed back into the forest. Impalas grazed in front of us and then walked gracefully down to the water. These antelope are prey to so many predators that they are always alert. Their delicate, neat bodies are poised so that with one elegant leap they can escape sharp claws and teeth. Although we now see them every day, we still stop and stare and wonder how anything could be that intensely beautiful.

After our picnic we went on a game drive, and what a drive it was. We saw a

family of black-backed jackals in the distance and went to investigate. They were jumping up, twisting in the air to catch hundreds of termites flying out of their mound. Carmine bee-eaters joined the jackals. The bee-eaters are nimble, multi-coloured birds with arrow-shaped tails; they flashed vivid red, purple green streaks as they dive-bombed the poor termites with exquisite grace. We were mesmerised by the swirl of colours and shapes dancing in front of our eyes.

Later we were driving on, delighted by what we had seen, when we heard a hissing noise coming from the front of the car. We had a flat tyre – wow, a real puncture! It took us thirty minutes to figure out how to work the high-lift jack.

Mum was convinced that we were all going to lose fingers in the jack mechanism, and her language was unrepeatable. We were sweating, huffing and puffing, but all that didn't matter. Eventually we succeeded in changing our first tyre by ourselves. As I look back on that day it seems ridiculous, changing tyres is a regular occurrence now, and achieved in less than ten minutes.

Once the tyre was changed, it was getting very late so we decided to head back home. The journey was well under way when we almost bumped into a herd of about six hundred buffaloes. We parked in the middle of the herd and just sat there listening to the lowing sounds they made. Most people do not like the way buffaloes smell but I adore it: they smell almost sweet, like cows. Then all of a sudden they bolted across the open plain and into the forest. When six hundred buffaloes stampede right past you they make an awesome noise. But the real thrill was wondering what had caused them to run. Mum said that she heard lions, but we didn't believe her.

Then three female lions with six tiny cubs came out of the bush, and everyone in the car fell silent. The lions lay down on the road, but the cubs were slightly more cautious. They came out slowly, watching us the whole time, but in a few minutes they were happily playing with each other. We had been going to the bush for many months and had never seen any lions, not because they were not there but because our eyes were not properly tuned. I really cannot explain how excited or how scared I felt. I knew how privileged I was to be able to see such special animals with their cubs right in front of me. After a while the lions moved off, their fragile cubs following behind them, taking at least four steps for every one step their mothers were taking. Since they headed in the direction of the buffaloes we assumed they were hunting, but they looked very relaxed about it. As we left them and headed home, how could we have known that these very lions would become a major part of our lives? In fact, the first lion I radio-tracked by myself, a few years later, was one of those little cubs. That day had a big effect on the whole family, as we started to feel more involved in the new world we were living in.

After months of day-trips Mum became more confident and felt it was time to spend a night in the bush. On the morning of Angus's eleventh birthday we packed a picnic as normal, but we also hid a small bell tent and five sleeping bags under the seats. We headed out and stopped under a tree on an open plain to unpack the car. When we told Angus what was happening, his face lit up. We set up the tent, which was a laugh, because we had never put one up before, but in the end it did not look too strange. Angus built the fire, and Mum cooked a vegetarian stew (we have been vegetarian all our lives). As it got dark everyone settled in around the fire, but this was hard for Oakley because he could not keep still for more than five minutes. Angus was opening his presents when we heard a strange noise, which sounded a little like a zebra. We hopped into the car to try to find where it was coming from, using the new spotlight that Angus had just unwrapped. We had not gone far when we picked up the glow of many eyes in the distance. Driving closer, we discovered a pack of fourteen African Wild Dogs, an endangered species. The dogs look like they have been painted with patches of white, yellow, brown and black. They have skinny legs and huge, rounded ears, and since they live in packs, are awesome predators. The dogs were coming back from a kill, and one of them was still carrying the head of an impala. They played around the car for a long time before they set off again. And when we turned off the spotlight everyone, except me, was in tears.

When we got back to our small camp we gave Angus his main present, a massive Swiss army knife with everything on it including a watch. Sadly it was stolen a few months later. We all huddled into bed and listened to the night sounds. Around midnight, a clan of hyenas killed an impala. The noise was eerie and soon we heard lions calling in the distance, yet even in those days I felt safe. Mum, however, did not. Before going to sleep Angus had been telling us gory stories about hyenas breaking into tents and eating people's faces. This did not help Mum, and while we were sleeping soundly beside her, she was on guard by the door of the tent, clutching Angus's new knife. We woke up refreshed in the morning, but Mum was a wreck. We were all very proud of ourselves however – we had survived. We broke camp, cleared up every scrap of rubbish and set off home. Angus marked it as one of his best birthdays. From then on we spent more and more nights out in the bush. We all loved it there and would often go to escape from town. It was on one of these trips that we first met Pieter; he was radio-tracking a lion…

MEETING PIETER AND THE LIONS

ANGUS

WE HAD SEEN PIETER around town and because he was a lion researcher, we kids had always wanted to meet him and discover what he actually did. We had also seen him on TV once, when staying at a hotel on a trip to the dentist. Mum and Pieter shared friends in town and we bumped into him again soon after our brief meeting in the bush. But we had little hope of getting to know him, as Mum was so determinedly independent. Then one day he invited us to Santawani Camp, which was the base for his research on lions. At first, Mum said she did not want to invade his camp with so many kids, but I think it was because she had sworn there would never be another man in her life. However, we soon managed to persuade her.

So one weekend we made the trip to the Lion Research Camp. We had taken the road many times before and were enjoying the scenery so much that we soon lost concentration. About twenty minutes from Pieter's camp, we took a wrong turn and got lost. After travelling along a muddy track we also got very stuck. It was the worst kind of mud, we call it black cotton mud, and the tyres just slipped around without traction. After two hours of digging, lying under the car, getting covered from head to toe in mud, and wedging blankets and Oakley's t-shirts under the tyres (we couldn't find any wood nearby) we had still made no progress. Mum was exhausted but Oakley, in his element, gathered armfuls of wild sage to put under the tyres, looking more and more like a child in *Lord of the Flies*. It was frustrating, as we knew we were so close to Santawani, Pieter's camp. To our huge relief two Gametrackers vehicles came by. They are a grand

I liked Pieter from the first moment I met him. He is kind, funny and energetic in a laid-back way.

safari company and when they saw how stuck we were they laughed a lot, but said they would be happy to pull us out. They were loath to get their smart uniforms dirty, but as we were filthy anyway, we happily dived back under the car to attach the chains. However, our problems were not over as one of their cars became stuck as well. It looked as if we might soon have a daisy chain of cars strung across the bush. Eventually we tied the Gametrackers vehicles together and linked them to our car with a tow-rope. All the cars drove at once and with a huge sucking sound we were pulled free. After many thank-you's we drove off and finally found Pieter's camp.

We arrived, completely filthy and sweaty, only to find that he wasn't there. Mum immediately said that it was too late to arrive at somebody's camp and that we should turn back straight away. We, knowing she meant differently, said that we had gone to too much trouble to go back now. Oakley begged, Travers started to unload the car and, fortunately, at that moment Pieter arrived. He was very welcoming and too polite to mention our revolting state. Mum cracked open a bottle of champagne and we settled in. It was getting late, and Pieter said that we should be quick if we wanted to see the lions he had found earlier. After a wonderful twenty-minute drive in his battered 2F Land Cruiser station wagon we came across the lions. It was remarkable to see the cats with someone who knew them well; he could tell us all their stories and who was related to whom. And I had never seen lions so close before. They were only about ten metres away and

from there we could see every little detail on their bodies. Pieter explained that the five cubs in front of us belonged to Amarula, Sauvignon and Cabernet. After much discussion we came to the conclusion that these must have been the lions we had seen hunting buffaloes all those months before, when the cubs were tiny. We were told to keep quiet so as not to disturb the lions. This was hard because we were pushing and shoving each other to get a better look. And Oakley, who was still a toddler, was so happy to see lions that he couldn't keep his mouth shut.

Suddenly, a kudu walked out of the forest. All the adult lions jumped up and started stalking, lying low to the ground, and then they burst out of the bushes and charged the antelope. Unfortunately for the lions the kudu was too fast for them and got away. At that time I thought the kudu was lucky but, having seen so many failed hunts, I have learned that lions catch only a small percentage of the prey they chase. After that first adventure we made regular trips to Santawani and began to learn more about Pieter and the Lion Research Project.

When we met Pieter he had been working with the lions for one and a half years. He came to Botswana from Kenya, where he had been researching African Wild Dogs and jackals, and doing genetic studies on different species of antelopes. He'd had discussions with the Botswana Wildlife Department and they had said that lion research was a top priority in the Delta. By then lions had been studied for thirty years in the Serengeti and other parts of Africa, and Pieter thought that much was already known about these cats. Due to outbreaks of canine distemper in the Serengeti that killed over one thousand lions, Pieter decided to concentrate the research on disease threats.

By the time we came into his life Pieter had pretty much sorted out who was who in the prides and where their territories were. He and Mum would talk deep into the night fuelled by their shared love of evolutionary biology, and more and more questions began to form in his mind. He began to question what had been written on lions and soon realised that much about their biology was still unknown.

At the beginning we children pressured Mum to take us to his camp. I think that she was reluctant to go because she knew that her friendship with Pieter could grow into something more and she was scared. But despite this, even though she said she would 'never be with a man again', my mother and Pieter fell in love. We spent many nights at Santawani and grew to love the area even more

A young Kudu browsing with its mother.

as our knowledge of the animals expanded. At this time we were living in the crocodile farm and it was from here that we took one of the biggest steps of our lives. Pieter asked us to move into the bush and live with him at Santawani – to exchange our reed walls for canvas and to come and live with the lions in the fresh air and wide open spaces.

I was excited but also a little surprised when Mum told us the news. I had liked Pieter from the first moment I met him but they had kept their romance very private and I did not know how serious it had become. He is very kind, funny and energetic in a laid-back way. He has always been willing to do things with us and, as he has three kids of his own (Philippa, Frieda, and Marieke, who live in America with their mother Lucy), he could cope with our continual demands and questions. Oaks, Maisie and I soon got used to the idea of Mum and Pieter being together, but Travers took much longer to feel comfortable with the change in our life. He wanted to be a hundred per cent sure that Pieter was going to be good to her. Our father is a good and honourable man who has always treated our mother well and he didn't want anything less for her. Even though Mum and Dad wanted to lead very different lives, they have always been close. Trav took his time but eventually found that Mum was in safe hands. Living with a stepfather was not a new concept to us, as Dad is Emily's stepfather and he loves her as much as all of us. We all have been lucky enough to have the same kind of parenting from Pieter who treats us as his own. Sadly we know how rare this is.

Our decision to move to Santawani did not just mean that we were going to live with Pieter, it meant that Mum would start to work with him as well. We children were given the chance to become an integral part of the project, which we all found thrilling. Mum's passion and commitment to understanding the complexities of the lion's reproductive system fired Pieter's interest and has lead them both to some exciting discoveries. Coming to live in the bush was a huge responsibility for Mum: not only was she going to be bringing us up in a tough environment and teaching us but also she had undertaken the massive task of working with wild lions.

During our brief time in Santawani we made friends with another exceptional person. His name is Witness and he is completely blind. He had measles when he was eight and lost his sight. He had a very hard life until the safari company that owns Santawani employed him as a gardener. He had to supply the camp with fresh vegetables. This was difficult, not only because of the climate but also because baboons and porcupines would eat his produce. But against all odds he created a garden that became famous far and wide and ended up providing all the Gametrackers camps with vegetables. Over the years he learned the layout of the camp by heart. He can stand anywhere on the premises and accurately point to the airstrip, the road to Maun, and every chalet or tree on the compound. After some time he was promoted to manager and the garden was taken over by the bush. No one else had his magic touch and capacity to nurse each plant and protect them from the elements.

However, being blind in the bush is extremely dangerous, as lions, leopards and elephants regularly walk through camp. This is where Witness's friends Sam and Dilao came in. Sam is a quiet, lean, lugubrious man, whilst Dilao is more sanguine with a permanent smile on his face. They are Witness's eyes at all times and gently guide him when animals are close by. They maintain the camp with great diligence and patiently repair water pipes that the elephants dig up day after day. When we were staying at Santawani, Oakley would 'help' them to cut the grass and clear leaves each day. They never tired of his constant chatter and endless energy, quietly getting on with their own thing as he pottered around with them.

Sadly we had to leave Santawani after only a few months because Gametrackers wanted to reopen the camp for tourists. We moved to a small camp on the Gomoti river, where we live now, but we still get our drinking water at Santawani and love to see Witness who tells us where the lions have been calling in the night. He has 'felt' Oakley grow up over the years and we still miss Santawani and our friends there.

THE MOVE AND THE BEGINNING
OF OUR LIFE IN THE BUSH

MAISIE

I FOUND IT QUITE HARD MOVING to the bush because I was leaving all my friends and the much-loved croc farm. But soon my passion for the bush overcame that sorrow and Mum promised that we could go into town a lot to see our friends. She kept this promise by driving back and forth at all hours of the day and night.

It was a big mission moving all our things into Gomoti camp. Sleeping in a tent is okay, but I miss walls to hang my pictures on, and the wind is always blowing my things off the tables and smashing them to pieces. Great! It was a beautiful camp even then but it was smaller than it is now. The kitchen was in a meru tent, just like in the film *Out of Africa*, with lots of pots and things hung on the tree outside. The veranda was our living room and dining room. All our strange sofas came with us and it was very comfortable. In those days Angus, Oakley and I shared a very colourful tent divided into two rooms. Mum and Pieter had their own tent and so did Travers. Months later Angus and I got our own tents which was really good. Oakley still sleeps with one or other of us; he is used to sleeping with the whole family. We now have a bed in the new kitchen tent and he sleeps beside us all as we sit at the table in the evening. The kitchen is just a huge fly-sheet with canvas walls on two sides.

We had a bucket shower in those days. It was hard to get used to, as all my life I had had running water and a flush loo. A bucket shower is a canvas bucket that has a showerhead connected to the bottom of it. The bucket is attached to a pulley system which means you can lever the bucket up and down, and fill it with hot water that has been heated by fire, in metal containers. We also had a 'long drop', which Emily called the 'drop pit'. This was a huge hole in the ground with a hippo pelvis loo seat on it. Fortunately we now have a proper wooden loo seat – the hippo was miserably uncomfortable.

THE DROP PIT

The drop pit is a huge hole where
   maggots feast on human poo.
Out of this stench the flies flew.
We live in the bush,
   so we don't have a flush loo.
But when we sit
   we look at the sky of blue.
You sit listening
   to the birds singing,
While the flies and maggots are milling,
And the drop pit you are filling.
The drop pit is not much fun,
I can assure you, you won't be there for long.

We used the bucket shower for a year and then Pieter and Mum fixed up a brilliant hot water system, with a barrel and a pump, and a hot water geyser. Heaven. But we still have the long drop!

Our camp has no fences, so the bush is basically our enormous back garden. Animals walk in and out of camp all the time, sometimes lions brush past our tents at night, and elephants feed on the nearby trees. It took me longer than the others to get used to the bush because I felt everyone was racing ahead of me. They knew the names of all the birds and insects and, though I could recognise them, I didn't always know what they were called. Also they were stronger than I was, so they could change tyres, use high-lift jacks and carry very heavy water containers. But I was able to drive.

Mum taught us how to drive on the old airstrip near Santawani. When I was behind the wheel I felt liberated and it wasn't long before I was driving Mum around the bush. One day I took Mum on a drive, and was feeling very happy about the way I was driving, when I turned a corner and came face to face with a big bull elephant. I slammed on the brakes and suddenly all of the stories I had

Like
lions
leopards
try
to avoid
getting
wet!

heard about elephants smashing cars to a pulp came to mind. My heart was racing, we must have surprised him as much as he surprised us and he started to run towards the car. Mum told me to slide the car into reverse but I stalled. She then banged very hard on the door of the car, which made the elephant falter. Then Mum told me to shift into first and *go for it*. We whizzed past the elephant and escaped safely. I felt proud.

The thing I like least about the bush is that you can't walk freely. In England I used to explore the fields and forests but here I can't because of the dangerous animals outside. All I want to do is go exploring, and ironically I feel trapped inside the camp boundaries.

What I like best is getting to know the insects and all the small things you don't see on a game drive. One day I watched a wandering spider, in the light of the car, stalk a rose beetle. Eventually the spider pounced on it, sinking its fangs in deep, and after a short while the beetle died. The wandering spider did not eat the external skeleton, but sucked the beetle's insides out leaving the shell behind. Wandering spiders mostly feed on lizards and geckos. They are about twenty-five millimetres in length and have a leg span of ninety millimetres. My favourite insects are termites: they are not the most magnificent animals

to look at but I find them very interesting. Termites look like orangey-yellowy ants with long abdomens, nothing spectacular. They are eusocial; this is a very unusual form of sociality because not all members of the group are reproductive. The young are not looked after by their parents but are taken care of by other members of the colony, which may belong to different generations.

Termites are very useful because they eat the dead grass and help to make way for new shoots. As I write I can see the termites flying. Yesterday we had torrential rain, and the termites have come out of their different mounds for their wedding flight. Once they have found a mate, they will lose their wings and start digging in the soft, damp soil to start new colonies. It's fascinating when the termites first come out. At night it's hard to cook because they get attracted to the light and fly into our food. In the morning the kitchen floor is covered in little wings and you can see the new couples burying themselves in the sand. The male stays with the female and helps her to build the new termite 'mountain' as Oakley calls it. They mix their saliva with sand and over

the years can build huge mounds of all different shapes and sizes, some of which can be over ten feet tall. A termite mound is like an iceberg, as you only see the tip and three-quarters of it is underground. The mounds have lots of tunnels, which form a type of air conditioning. Inside the hot air rises and flows through holes in the mound and cool air comes in through tunnels at the bottom.

This is perfect. Right in front of me I can see two huge termite mushrooms that Pieter has just found and left on the kitchen table. Let me tell you about these mushrooms.

Termites eat vegetable matter, which is very hard to digest because of the cellulose, so they build combs out of their semi-digested pellets. These become a

A termite mound is like
an iceberg, you can only
see the tip.

BELOW Underneath the
ground there are lots of
tunnels which form a type
of air-conditioning system.

Angus and Oakley sitting
on a termite 'mountain'.

mushroom farm. The tiny mushrooms grow well because the pellet chambers are dark and humid. They help break down the pellets and then the termites eat the broken-down comb. After the rains the mounds become soft and the tiny mushrooms underground turn into huge mushrooms which burst out into the open. Termite mushrooms are delicious; this rainy season we have had them nearly every night and we haven't got sick of them. This is my favourite recipe for them:

GARLIC TERMITE MUSHROOMS

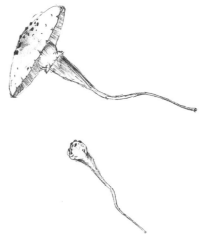

INGREDIENTS
Termite mushrooms, garlic, butter, soy sauce and Gruyère cheese.

METHOD
Chop up the mushroom stalks into thick slices (the stalks are my favourite, people who eat meat say they taste like chicken), then slice the caps (they are slimier and soggier than the firm caps, I don't like them as much).
Fry up the stalks in a lot of butter, garlic and soy sauce. They will absorb the liquid and turn crisp and brown. Then fry the caps separately, they will make more liquid and you can use this as a sauce to dunk bread into. Or you could put whole caps on a baking tray and sprinkle them with garlic butter, soy sauce and grated Gruyère cheese. Then bake them in a medium oven until they are cooked and golden brown.

Eat with chunks of brown bread, red wine and crisp green salad!

(Remember it doesn't need to be termite mushrooms, any kind of mushroom is fine, but termite mushrooms are the best.)

Try it!

TERMITE MOUND WITH TERMITE MUSHROOM
BY MAISIE   GROWING OUT OF IT

The other day Travers found a mushroom that was as tall as Oakley and the stem was thicker than Travers's head. Sadly it was full of beetle maggots so we couldn't eat it. We have found many unexpected things to enjoy since we have moved to camp, like this enormous termite mushroom, but there have also been drawbacks.

I missed our dogs a lot. Sadly we couldn't bring them to the bush, as a leopard, lion or another predator would probably have eaten them and they could have

spread diseases among the wild animals. Zambo at the croc farm took Oakley's dog Simba and we found homes for some of the others, but horribly we had to put three down, as no one wanted them. I still feel terrible about that. We now have a pet squirrel in camp, named Squiddle, who we all love dearly. Before we had her we had some rather unusual pets. I have always been desperate to have an animal of my own but the only ones I could find out here were either wounded or dying.

When we moved to join Pieter, the first pets I had (well they weren't pets really), were a collection of snails. I had about ten of them in a small tank, and they were actually quite interesting because they were mating and laying eggs, but unfortunately I left them in the sun one day and they all fried. I also had five freshwater clams that I kept in a bowl in my tent. I would give them water from a pan every other day and I named them after the Spice Girls (please, you must remember I was very young at the time). Sadly they died too.

The next pet I had was a leopard tortoise. Pieter found it on the road and brought it home for me. We called him Leo. He was all beaten up and had one eye missing. Pieter and Angus thought Matabele ants must have attacked him. These are huge, black, aggressive, carnivorous ants that bite your toes; the pain they inflict can last for days. I looked after Leo for two weeks, feeding him on fruit and vegetables. I had to be careful as he might have been carrying salmonella. We fed him and played with him, but one day he stayed in the same position for hours. I found this quite weird, so I picked him up only to discover he was dead too. Great! All these pets dying upset me, so I gave up for a while.

About a year went by and I really wanted a new pet, when one morning Travers found a baby dove outside the kitchen tent. I was excited and rushed to see it. We looked closely and discovered it had fallen out of an acacia tree and had been scalped by the sharp thorns on a palm bush. Travers picked up the shocked baby dove and sat on the sofa and began to stroke it. I begged to hold it and he gave it to me. I felt so sorry for the bird and put it in a box Angus had prepared by lining it with a flannel. Some time later Mum came back from finding the lions and I asked her if I could look after it. She said 'of course' but warned me there wasn't much hope. Angus and I made a drink of mashed-up peaches, water and digestive biscuits. The dove absolutely loved it and gulped it down. That evening as it became cold and dark I made up a hot-water bottle and put the dove to sleep in my tent. After supper we watched a video, but when I went to bed I found the dove lying there as stiff as a brick. I wasn't surprised, as I knew it would probably die soon, but I was again very disappointed. At least the poor thing died warm and comfortable.

Weeks later, guess what? We found another dove in exactly the same place. We found the nest and assumed the young birds had fallen out while fighting for their food and their parents' attention. This dove was bigger than the previous one so we hoped it might survive with a little help. That afternoon I left it with Travers while Angus and I went to Santawani to collect water. We have to drive seven kilometres to get our clean drinking water from a borehole. It's a lovely drive, and we were chatting away and listening to music when Travers radioed through to say the dove had just died. We were very upset but not that surprised as it had been quite badly wounded in the fall.

Months later I was in town staying with my best friend Lena when someone told me they had just seen Mum, Pieter, Emily and Oakley nursing a baby impala. I thought he was joking but he assured me it was true. He had seen the impala with an intravenous drip in its leg lying in our kitchen. Mum nursed it through the night but all their efforts couldn't save it and by the time I got home it was dead. I will let Oakley tell you this part of our story as he was there:

66 One morning in the year two thousand, Gabby and Nafatse (they have been with us for years and help us in camp) rushed up to the tent and said there was a baby impala next to the long drop. Me, Mum and Pieter rushed very fast, we saw the impala, it was screaming out. Mum picked her up and quickly took her to the mess tent. We lay her down on a blanket and gave her an injection to give her water. We lay down and cuddled her, and we decided to call her Milly. That day we went out for a game drive to find the lions and had to leave Milly behind. I couldn't stay with her because nobody was in camp and it was very dangerous if I

stayed in camp by myself. I wasn't very happy because I couldn't stay behind with Milly. When we came back she was better but she still couldn't walk.

That night we had to go to Santawani Camp, because it was New Year's Eve, and listen to a Marimba band from Maun Secondary School. I loved the Marimba band a lot, and my favourite song was Kumbaya. I sang it a lot of times in our camp and every one thought it was very bad. After that we went back home to check Milly and she was fine under her blanket.

Then we went out again to have the exact moment of the year two thousand on an open plain and had crepe suzettes. I must explain what crepe suzette is. You fry a pancake and then you put brandy in it and put a lighted match to the pancake and the brandy, and a flame comes up. I was with my eldest sister Emily and Pieter, and Mum made me a little bed on the sand and we looked at the sky. It was very black because it was going to rain, there was not a star or a moon in sight. Just as the moment came, a lightning struck and Pieter said the world will end and he cracked open a bottle of champagne and we all had a glass. Even me and I'm only six years old. We went back to camp to find Milly was better and Mum spent all night with her and fed her all night.

The next morning one eye was blind and I shouted to Pieter 'she's not breathing'. He pumped her heart and then very sadly she died. Pieter was so sad and just as Mum came back from collecting the water he rushed to her and told her Milly was dead. Everyone was very sad and did not know what to do with her. But suddenly Mum said there is only one thing to do and that is to hang her up in a tree for a leopard. It was very scary because as Pieter put her up on the car her puke started to dribble down the windscreen. And we tied her up the tree and her puke went on to the bonnet. We rushed home and Pieter took a whole bowl of water and told us to wind up the windows as he poured it all over the car.

We didn't get a leopard from Milly but something small like a genet nibbled at her. It took a long time for her to be eaten. It was much better for us to hang her up than bury her because we want to feed the animals and we don't want them to starve.

Milly died because she was very sick and her parents would have abandoned her because they didn't want any of the other impalas to get sick. I was very sad she died because it would have been lovely if she could get up and walk off and come back and we could stroke her.

Now I am very happy because we have a pet squirrel who is fine. And she is still alive right now when I am speaking.

We got Squiddle from Corrie and Anne (they are the managers of Croc Camp, a tourist camp near us). Squiddle's mother had somehow died and he needed to be fed. We fed him milk, a tiny bit of honey and an egg through a pipette, and he loved it a lot. He needed to be fed every two hours until he was big enough to eat food. He loves apple and little crumbles of bread. And he also loves nibbling on garlic and olives. He does very funny things, he has just walked over the computer and typed a number four, we had to take it out but he will definitely do it again. He is very clever and can open zips on our tents. This morning he woke Travers very early by coming into his tent and biting his toes. Travers was very cross because he had had a very late night. He had been to rescue Kate (a student who works on our project) because she was very stuck in a pan. A pan is like a big puddle, and when it's dry it is just lots of dried up mud, but Travers, Angus and Pieter got stuck themselves eleven times trying to get her out. They got home at six-thirty in the morning and Travers was very tired. Squiddle puts himself to bed all by hisself at five o'clock in the afternoon. I do never do that because it is too dangerous to walk by yourself once it starts to get dark. He used to sleep in Travers's tent but now he has moved into my tent with Maisie and Angus, he sleeps in our bed. I am very bursting to leave, so good night, and Maisie will tell you the rest. 🙶

Squiddle thinks that we are his family and our tents are his territory, and I hope with all my heart that once he gets older he stays, but most probably he will move out to have a family. I have loved all of my eccentric pets but most of all I love the lions.

Over the first few months Pieter taught us about the lions and who was who in every pride. Now we know all of them well and spend hours watching them, especially in the evenings when we go out with Mum to 'poop' the lions. When we first moved to Africa we never guessed that we would end up so closely attached to lions. It took us a long time to learn about them and a lot of extraordinary things happened on the way.

CHAPTER THREE **THE LION CHILDREN**

LEARNING THE ROPES

ANGUS

WHEN WE FIRST MOVED to join Pieter, lions were simply lions. They all looked the same and anything we knew about them was gleaned from the field guides Mum had bought us. Now we have developed a rich understanding about them and have learned to know and love each individual so much that we cannot imagine life without them. Becoming that intimate with the animals was a tremendous challenge, but I think one of the hardest things was, and still is, learning the area that the lions live in, or 'study area', as we soon came to know it.

Lions have huge territories that can cover hundreds of square kilometres and with five prides to study, it was a monumental task to learn the lie of the land. Miraculously Travers only took about two weeks to learn most of the roads. Mum was next, followed by Maisie, and I who have an appalling sense of direction, lagged far behind. To this day I often don't have a clue where I am. Travers and Pieter taught us the names of each landmark; they are named after events, like Eland Kill Pan, where Pieter found the Santawani pride eating an eland, Leopard Corner, or Elephant Hunt Mound, where we interrupted a trophy hunter who was about to shoot an elephant in an area where hunting is restricted. Travers can't explain how he knows his way around: he just sees shapes and outlines in the tree lines, he is familiar with every termite mound and knows the contours of the dried up pans in the dust. It is as if he has a private map inside his head. However, as lions spend most of their time in thick scrub or in forests, learning the landmarks on the roads was only half the story.

In this varied environment, with a multitude of habitats from acacia woodland, palm scrub and savannah to flood plains and riverine forest, it is impossible to find the lions without a tracking device. Key lions in each pride are fitted with radio collars, these send out radio signals that we can pick up with a receiver and antenna. Pieter taught Mum how to track and at first it looked like any fool could do this, but we soon found out how complicated tracking can be. In the early days Mum went out with us kids and learned the hard way. One of the main problems is bouncing radio waves. If a lion is lying behind a termite mound, or is walking through a forest, the signal can get bounced off obstacles and can send you on a wild goose chase.

We discovered this while tracking a pride male called Bordeaux. We had picked up his signal and it sounded like he was in a thick forest to our left. We veered off the beaten track and as the signal became stronger we thought he must be only a few metres away. However, after half an hour of driving round in circles we had still not found him. Soon the frustration became too great and reluctantly we decided to give up. As we came back on to the road we were flabbergasted to see Bordeaux calmly gazing at us, oblivious to our struggle, relaxing in the shade of a massive termite mound right by the side of the road. The termite mound had diverted the signal and sent us hurtling into the forest.

The signal is not the only problem we have while tracking, the stuff the lions go into sometimes seems impossible. The Santawani pride are forest lions and they have put us in some very tricky situations over the years. Leadwood trees have branches armed with three-inch thorns that can slice through tyres like a hot knife through butter. Thick mopane woodland is almost impenetrable and camelthorn forests have deadly logs hidden beneath long grass. We have often been in situations where logs have got wedged between the car axles and we can't move forward or backwards. I remember once trying to dig out a colossal branch from underneath the car, and in desperation attempting to saw it in half with a pocket-knife. Walking home was not an option with the lions close by, and it took hours of huffing and puffing to

Pieter radio-tracking for lions.

dig out the log. When we told Pieter he laughed a lot and taught us a more effi-
cient method using the high-lift jack.

Despite all the struggles, when you get to the lions, it is always worthwhile. I
admit, some days aren't as exciting as others; a lot of the time the lions are just
lying under a bush sleeping, not moving for hours on end. Sometimes we bring
games like backgammon and draughts to entertain ourselves. But they are fascinating, it's not just their behaviour that interests us, but who they are associating
with, what condition they're in and where they are in relation to other lions.
Most of these questions would seem boring if we didn't know the lions as well as
we do. A stranger coming upon a mating pair might assume that it was a pride
male mating with one of his females, they would not assume that it was in fact a
female 'cheating' on her pride male and mating with a male from a neighbouring
territory. We were very intrigued when we witnessed this because the female was
cuckolding the pride male, but also because the resulting cubs were accepted by
the pride male as his own.

At first, learning the lions' names seemed a Sisyphean task, as Pieter had named
them all after wines! Some were unpronounceable like Freixenet (Freyshenet) or
Haut Brion. Our prides range in numbers from about thirteen to thirty-three
lions and we study five prides – that's a lot of wine. But over time we learned to
recognise them all. Not by 'knowing' their faces, this is a sentimental and unreliable means of identifying a lion but by looking at them in detail.

Identifying a lion is complicated but I found it fascinating to learn. Each lion
has its own unique whisker pattern, like humans have fingerprints. The whisker
pattern is a sequence of dots where the whiskers come out of their cheeks; they
have many rows of dots on their muzzles but we focus on the top row which
consists of six to eight dots. Above and below this line there are random spots
that form a distinct pattern. We map this pattern in our precious whisker-pattern
book, and by using this method we have now identified over three hundred lions
in the Okavango Delta.

There are several other characteristics that we map, such as ear notches. Lions
get cuts and nicks in their ears by walking through dense bush or in fights, and
they can be very helpful clues. Teeth can also tell us a lot, as they yellow with
age, and we note missing and chipped canines or incisors. One female in the
Gomoti pride has no bottom teeth at all and sucks at the guts on a kill; she has
survived for five years like this. As Mum spent more and more time with the
lions she noticed another very useful ID marker. Some lions may have dark
patches on their gums in front of or behind their incisors; these are very dis-
tinctive and have helped us to confirm uncertain IDs many times. Spots on
their irises and scars are also helpful, but scars are unreliable as they fade over

time. We need to observe the iris spots of the cubs we are following to see if they are reliable indicators or if they too change over time.

As you can imagine, identifying a lion is time consuming and it is very important to stay absolutely still in the car while it is taking place. Poor Oakley is constantly being told to sit tight and stop wriggling, which after anything up to five hours in the car can be tough for a six year old. But he has absorbed, as if by osmosis, much information and has developed a very sharp eye. Oakley won his colours one day in 1998, not with an ID but simply by counting accurately.

That year the Santawani pride had eleven cubs and they were all doing very well, until one day we were disturbed to find that one cub was missing. After three weeks and still only finding ten cubs with the females we concluded the cub must be dead. Then one afternoon while we were sitting with the pride waiting for them to poop (Travers will explain about this later), we heard a little voice pipe up from the back: 'Eleven, there's eleven cubbies'. We looked at Oakley in disbelief and were convinced he must have miscounted. But Oakley was adamant and when we discovered to our joy that he was right, he nearly burst with pride. This was a huge lesson because we had all assumed that we would never see the cub again and had not counted the cubs ourselves. We will never know how such a little cub survived alone, but since then we have seen young cubs eating francolins, the bush equivalent of a chicken, and a mongoose, a ferret-like mammal, so we have to assume that she managed this way. On Oakley's sixth birthday he was given his own grown-up binoculars, which he uses with great skill.

Our family has acquired very sharp eyes but not all sightings are so joyous. One of the saddest identifications we have ever done was on a lion named Shiraz. I remember the first time I saw Shiraz. It was a hot day and we were tracking for him through some dense bush. Then suddenly he rose out of the sage and looked at us with his warm amber eyes. He strolled away from us, his great bulk swaying from side to side, his powerful forearms ploughing through the tawny grass, muscles bulging along the way. Shiraz was an old lion, with broken teeth and a scarred nose, but he was still magnificent, with a mane as rich as wild honey and as dark as the night sky. When you looked into his face you could see his internal beauties: courage, nobleness, greatness, gentleness, strength, rage and love. When they both lay together, their manes glinting in the sun, Shiraz and his companion Merlot looked invincible, so powerful, so huge that you thought nothing could break the bond between them.

The day we found Shiraz' skull lying in the grass I was heartbroken. The remains of his mane flowing around the ground like feathers was one of the saddest sights I have ever seen. We had been following a very strong signal for an

hour, going round and round in circles, when Mum caught sight of the skull out of the corner of her eye. 'It's a kill,' she cried, but as we drove nearer Pieter whispered 'It's Shiraz'. He had recognised the familiar blunted right canine in the bottom jaw. We had friends in the car at the time, which was quite hard because they could not know what his death meant to us.

We had no idea how Shiraz died, but we knew that Merlot would soon disappear, for without his partner he stood little chance in a challenge by other males.

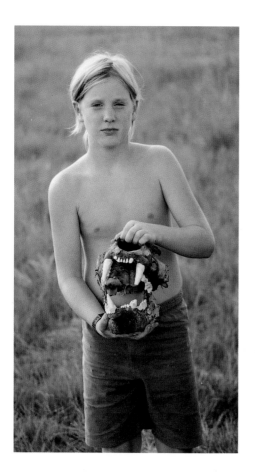

We were also very concerned for a female in his pride who had just given birth to a cub; it turned out that these concerns were justified as the cub disappeared. She could have been abandoned by her mother or killed by the new males that took over the pride a few months later (see Lion Fact File).

Fortunately few days are as sad. Every day is different and it is always hard to decide whether to stay in camp and risk missing something exciting, or to go out and slug around the bush only to find a sleeping lion. We each have our own regrets and triumphs related to these decisions. One adventure I'm glad I didn't miss happened during our early days. Mum and I went out, leaving everyone else in camp. We found Chandon, one of the Santawani females, mating with a nomadic male named Gascoigne. We were fascinated by this because the day before we had seen her shun one of the Santawani pride males when he tried to mate her. We were witnessing an opportunistic mating with a nomad and since we are very interested in the idea that nomads may indeed sire some of the cubs in a pride you can imagine how excited we were. As it turned out she was not fertilised during this mating, and did not become pregnant.

Chandon and Gascoigne were mating every ten minutes or so and we stayed with them for hours, hoping to collect a poop. Lions rarely poop while mating and we were giving up hope as the light began to fade. Gascoigne's partner Gigondas had been lying nearby all day and finally got bored and left to go hunting. We decided to come back in the morning. Lions can mate for days at a time so we were reasonably sure we would find them again (for more on mating see Lion Fact File).

We set off confidently, leaving the forest behind us and heading for a road that lay a few kilometres away. We were chatting and laughing but after a while we grew somewhat concerned that the road was still not in sight. We came to a forest. 'Oh,' we said, 'this is interesting.' No problem, we could just turn around and start again. It is very hard driving off-road in the dark because you cannot see well enough to find your bearings. Our difficulties were exacerbated by the fact that both Mum and I are directionally challenged. We arrived back at the lions and looked for the tracks we had made coming in from the road. We could barely see them and lost them again quite quickly. We drove around in circles trying to find the tracks again, but kept driving off on tracks we had just made and turning into forests. It would have been very funny to watch us meandering around from the air. We had absolutely no idea where we were and as it was a cloudy night we couldn't use the GPS (Global Positioning System) because it couldn't locate any satellites. Mum hates the GPS like poison. She says it is useless in so many situations and she still swears by a compass, which we unfortunately did not have with us! However, we did know where the lions were, and we went back to them because Mum said that at least she could get some more data and I could sleep in the back of the car. Luckily we had some sandwiches and drinks in the fridge and fortunately the untidy Oaks had left his backgammon board in the car. We had a wonderful night yet we felt a tinge of anxiety about the others, as we knew they would be worrying about us. In those days we had no radios in the car so we couldn't call and put their minds at rest. Sure enough, after an hour or so we saw car lights in the distance. We assumed it was Pieter looking for us and waved our spotlight frantically to no avail. It was very frustrating to see the car lights circling around us and not being able to make contact. The lights eventually faded into the distance and the darkness deepened once more. We were pretty confident that Pieter would sensibly go home with the others and try to find us again at first light. Eventually I dozed off to the sound of lions roaring.

I woke up at dawn the next morning to hear the car engine. Peering through the windscreen I saw a track twenty metres in front of us – Mum had found the road! She said it was much easier in the light. On our way home we found two male cheetahs basking in the first light of the morning – it was like a reward for our night's frustration. When we arrived back in camp we found everyone about to embark on another search and rescue mission. When they saw us their faces relaxed and Oakley ran towards Mum and flung his arms around her. Over a huge breakfast we all talked at once and told our stories of the night before. Oakley adores a good rescue and to this day loves nothing more than digging out stuck cars. He had been cross that Pieter had wisely abandoned the mission and taken everyone home. Night driving can be treacherous and it is stupid to risk having two stuck cars. This was the beginning of many nights we have had to sleep in the bush due to one thing or another. However we now have radios in each vehicle and can call for help if we have any big problems.

This life's unpredictability is what I find exciting. I'm not going to lie to you and say everything about living here is wonderful, as Maisie will explain, but most things I wouldn't want to change for anything. As I'm writing I'm sitting in the middle of a huge storm, the tail end of a cyclone that has ravaged southern Africa. The Gomoti River is flowing for the first time in seven years and we can now fish from camp. Only last year we had a massive drought and the land was parched. The Okavango Delta is dynamic and wild, and after living out here for so long we have learned to take things as they come.

SETTLED IN

TRAVERS

NOVEMBER IS A TIME OF ANTICIPATION. The air is hot, and the dry wind picks up loose grains of sand and tosses them around chaotically. The termites carry away the last remaining stalks of brittle grass and pull them underground. The impalas walk across dry plains waiting for the smell of the first rains that will release succulent, tender shoots from the parched earth. The clouds gather and the sky turns from bright blue into dull grey, and then to pitch black within minutes. Thunder cracks the silent sky, and lightning strikes the ground. The rain starts slowly at first, but then it comes down with enormous force. Sheets and sheets of water are released from above. Incredibly, anything up to eighty millilitres of water can land in one spot within a few hours. Almost everyone in Botswana runs out of their house as soon as they hear the longed-for sound of the first drops of rain hitting the baked sand. People start laughing, singing, dancing and rejoicing, splashing in the rapidly forming puddles and dreaming of the lush new grass that will soon appear. From that moment there is only one subject of conversation: the rain, how much has fallen, how much they hope will continue to fall, how much fell last year, the joys of rain, rain and more rain.

Our family takes a slightly different view of the rainy season. As those first drops hit the ground, we all rush about pulling down flaps to prevent the tents from flooding, covering our precious books with blankets, throwing tarpaulins over generators and machinery, closing car windows, making sure all electrical equipment is put safely away, and all the while shouting instructions to each other. As the wind picks up, it collects under the roof of the mess tent and fills it out like a sail. We each grab hold of a tent pole, clinging on for dear life, as the rain lashes against our skin and the wind howls past our ears. Meanwhile Pieter stands in the middle of the tent calling out directions like the captain of a ship. At the end of the storm it is noticeable that Pieter is remarkably dry and cool, while we stand before him panting and soaked to the skin! When the rain finally abates we spend the next hour sweeping water out of the kitchen tent and looking for any damage. We then exchange our wet clothes for our merely damp clothes and admire the magnificent electric blue light that filters through the dark, retreating clouds.

The worst rainy season we experienced was between November 1999 and April 2000. The November rain was very gentle, and we all thought that it was going to be a regular wet season. Then two cyclones hit southern Africa in a short space of time, leaving almost a million people homeless and stranded (a woman had to give birth in a tree because she was cut off from all help). Hundreds died, and Mozambique's already weak infrastructure was destroyed. At one point Botswana was about to declare a state of emergency, as there was deep concern that the intense flooding would burst two dams in the populated eastern edge of the country. Maun wasn't hit so badly but the harsh reality struck close to home when we were told over the radio that Bring's house had been destroyed in a huge storm the night before. Bring, Olivia, Gabby and Nafatse have been with us for over two years and help us run the camp. Like many houses in Botswana, Bring's family home in Shorobe, thirty-five kilometres away, was made of termite mound bricks bound by water and cow's blood. With only a simple thatched roof to keep out the rain, his house literally dissolved and

In the year 2000 the Gomoti River flowed for the first time in seven years and we could fish from camp.

was swept away by water. We immediately drove him to his village so that he could relocate his family and start to make plans to build a new house. While we were very upset, Bring and his wife Grace appeared to be remarkably sanguine and took it all in their stride, in spite of the fact they had months of hard work ahead building a new house.

Despite a strong economy supported by diamond mining and other mineral resources, there is still a substantial amount of poverty in Botswana and many people cannot afford to build stronger houses. In the malaria season the small rural hospitals soon run out of bed space and as a result extremely sick and in some cases dying people have to sleep on the floors. In contrast to Mozambique and South Africa, Botswana was fortunate to receive only the tail end of the cyclones.

While our problems in camp seemed insignificant in comparison, our life was turned upside down by the rain. For two weeks it was almost impossible to find the lions as we continually had to dig ourselves out of seas of mud. We reached our nadir one night when the collection of a single poop sample caused us to get stuck eleven times! We had to dig and jack up the car all throughout the night in the pouring rain. At dawn we tottered into camp, sodden and exhausted, to be greeted by a very anxious mother. You may wonder why we had chosen not to sleep in the car and dig in the daylight. The mosquitoes were out with a vengeance that night and at one point the windscreen was literally blackened by them. Keeping active by digging was a much better option than being eaten alive while trying to sleep.

LEFT Travers driving home in the rainy season.

RIGHT A banded rubber frog.

It has been raining continuously for days now and I have been asking myself why we are not living in a comfortable house, and what we are achieving by living like this. I have been doing a lot of thinking lately and have come to realise that the lions are a kind of support to us. They are the reason we are here and despite the rain and the mud we are still curious to know what they are doing and how they are. Our love for them keeps us going, but in the end that is not enough. We have grown up a lot over the last three years and now know that understanding needs to be the driving force behind good conservation.

Most of us first learned about lions through reference books and TV documentaries. But by observing them and following their everyday stories we found that much of the information we had received was wrong. We have learned the hard way not to trust blindly all that we read and see. Let me give you some examples. Among other inaccuracies, one well-known children's encyclopaedia states: 'The females in a pride are usually sisters, and remain together all their lives.' In fact, the degree of relatedness within a pride depends on how related the pride males are (see Lion Fact File). Therefore, though some females may indeed be sisters or half sisters, aunts or cousins, some may not be genetically related. The degree of relatedness within a pride probably fluctuates from generation to generation. This encyclopaedia also states: 'The cubs are fed and looked after by their aunts as well as their mother.' Lions communally suckle their young, and females do not discriminate against cubs though they may be only distantly related to them or not related at all. Once they come out of their den, the cubs, like human children, have no means of knowing if members of their extended 'family' are genetically related. Cubs bond to others in their cohort by familiarity and these bonds last a lifetime. However, they may not spend their entire lives with their pride. Some females prefer a more solitary existence and others form peripheral groups. This is so much more interesting and complex than the neat picture that is so often presented.

For us every day is a biology lesson, and we are lucky enough not be solely dependent on dry textbooks, for we are being taught by nature itself. Mum and Pieter have brought genetics, evolution and reproductive biology alive, as these subjects are pivotal to our work with the lions. And each one of us is included in every aspect of project life (some less appealing than others). Not many children have the opportunity to make significant contributions to their parents' work. This can be a daunting responsibility at times. A few months ago, Mum and Pieter had gone to have a hard-earned break at a nearby camp, leaving us in the care of a good friend. In the morning I had taken her out on a game drive to find the Santawani lions. On the way back we came upon two young lions that I identified as Krystal and Freixenet. I was terribly excited as this meant these young females had moved back into the pride territory after a prolonged absence. Realising how important this was, I radioed Mum and Pieter to tell them the good news. They said they would come back immediately, as Krystal needed to be fitted with a radio collar. On hearing that, I felt very nervous and dearly hoped I hadn't made a mistake in the ID and ruined their holiday. They were very proud of me as I had got it right, and Pieter realised that his 'team' was becoming more and more effective.

A good understanding of lion reproduction is essential if wild lion populations are going to be managed sensibly (see Lion Fact File). Collecting poop is a non-invasive way of gathering data, as reproductive steroid hormones are voided in the faeces. We could do it by taking blood but that would mean having to immobilise the lion. Pooping the lions is a great family affair, and Mum loves it when we come with her, as we know the lions so well, and with anything up to twenty-one lions to work with we all need eyes in the back of our heads. We try to sample every day, and while we are waiting for them to 'go' we do our homework. Collecting the samples is not always very safe when the lions are nearby, and we have to keep a watchful eye on them while Mum is out of the car. During this time Oakley is an equal part of the team. Not many children could be trusted with such a responsibility and we are all very proud of him because he is utterly reliable. On the drive home the powerful smell lingers in the air and clings to you, and at times we feel like retching. When we get back to camp we store it in the fridge to keep it cool overnight. (In case you're wondering, we have a separate fridge for food!) The next day it is processed and later sent to the USA to be analysed.

It is still unclear how many lions there are left in Africa. Pieter believes it could be as few as 15,000. Did you know that in the Middle Ages it was difficult to find a place in the world where there were no lions? They roamed freely across Europe, Africa and Asia. But as human populations expanded, lions were relentlessly killed, since these powerful predators posed a great risk to livestock and humans. Lions have also been killed as part of manhood initiation ceremonies, and even to decorate floors and walls. As a result, lions are now confined to small, isolated pockets of Africa, and one forest in India. In spite of the fact that we do not know how many lions are left in Africa, they are still being killed as hunting trophies and 'problem animals'. Lions are not yet considered an endangered species but we have now reached a critical stage in their conservation and have to consider some very serious choices.

With this in mind, the Government of Botswana initiated a lion survey in 1998 that was to be run by the Department of Wildlife and National Parks (DWNP). The purpose of the survey was to try and establish how many lions there are in northern Botswana. The DWNP were worried about the number of lions being shot for trophies by hunters while they had such limited information about the size of the lion population. They also wanted to know more about population structure, so they asked independent researchers to run the survey together with members of the Wildlife Department. There were three teams that worked on the surveys, and Pieter, Angus and I formed one of them. This was a big responsibility and even though it is not directly part of our research we see it as very important. Outside southern Africa it is unclear how many lions are left on the continent and this survey is a positive start towards developing that understanding.

There has been much discussion about survey methods and, while no method is perfect, we have found that calling stations are most effective in this habitat. We literally call the lions to us by playing amplified tapes of buffaloes in distress and hyenas going crazy at a kill. Lions have exceptionally good hearing and can pick up the sound five kilometres away. We do three calling stations each night, which can get very tiring because we get to bed at around two thirty in the morning and have to do school in the morning. On the other hand it can be so exciting that, when we eventually get into bed, we can't sleep because the adrenaline is still pumping through our bodies.

As soon as the sun sets, we bundle all the equipment into the back of the car and head for the first calling station. We find a suitable tree in an open place and tie a piece of meat to it. (We use these baits because we need the lions to stay in one place long enough to photograph both sides of each lion's face in order to identify them properly.) We put up the speakers, slot the tape in and try to get comfortable before we sit absolutely still for the next hour and a half. By this time it is pitch black and the bush is full of noises: owls hooting, hyenas calling in the distance and jackals singing their whining song across the plains. Sometimes it can get quite freaky when you're sitting in a car in complete darkness listening to every blade of grass rustle and knowing that at any minute a pride of lions or a clan of hyenas could burst on to the scene.

When the first lion arrives everyone in the car springs to life, grabbing our binoculars, cameras and spotlight as this is when the action starts. The lions follow their noses trying to find the meat and we start counting and sexing them. This is not as simple as it sounds; often young males have no manes and are easily mistaken for females. Equally some females are very hairy and can be mistaken for sub-adult males. Pieter has taught Angus and me to work at lightning speed while at the same time being accurate. A mistake can have a negative effect on all the data we collect. As the lions home in on their meal, and pounce on the bait, we have to photograph and identify each lion before it gets covered in blood.

Identifying the lions is the most important part of the work; we have to note down whisker patterns and ear notches that we will later match with the photographs. Over the last three years we have identified hundreds of lions using this method. Taking photos of the lions is a tricky business and at times we have to get very close to them. We all work as if we were one body: Pieter mans the camera and flash, Angus writes down all the information as Pieter calls it out, and I operate the spotlight and keep tabs on each lion. It is important that Angus is one hundred per cent accurate during this time, so no one but Pieter talks.

We work quietly because some of the lions can be really shy. Some lions are fearless, however, and once a female ran right under the car almost taking Pieter's

As the sun set we would bundle all the equipment
in the car and head for the first calling station.

arm with her. When we have finished the IDs we try to recover the bait so we can use it at the next calling station. This can be quite dangerous, as lions are notoriously protective of their food. I have to shine the spotlight on the lions while Pieter and the wildlife officers try to untie the bait without the lions noticing.

Over the years we have made good friends with the wildlife officers but for some reason everyone is convinced my name is Charles. This has gone on for so long that I have almost come to believe it myself. Angus, miraculously, has acquired the names Hunger and Small French Boy, whilst Pieter, more reasonably, is simply known as Kat. Some nights can be very boring and there is a limit to how often you can hear the same buffalo-in-distress tape without going insane.

During the surveys we have learned to 'read' lions that are strange to us, and also how to make sensible decisions in potentially dangerous situations. There is no doubt it is a hazardous job but we know that it has great value. Botswana has one of the few truly free-ranging wild lion populations in Africa, and by combining survey results with results from our intensive research there is real hope that we can keep them safe.

However, we were shocked to learn that, in spite of Mum and Pieter's strong objections, the information collected during the survey was used to increase the trophy-hunting quota of lions in the Okavango area by 150 per cent! This is a catastrophe for the lions in Botswana, which I will talk about in Chapter 5.

LIFE IS HARD FOR A LION CUB

MAISIE

I AM CONSTANTLY SURPRISED by how hard a lion's life is. I had always thought that they were huge killing machines and that they could take on anything. But since I've come to know them I have realised there is more to them than that.

I am going to tell you about an amazing young female. She is not yet two and yet she is already the bravest lion I have known. We have named her Mercier, and Angus has already told you how she disappeared for two and a half weeks. She was seven months old at the time and only as big as a border collie. She was defenceless against hyenas, leopards and maybe even animals like buffaloes and elephants. Can you imagine how scared she must have been all alone in the bush? Oakley won't sleep in his tent alone even if we are up in the kitchen because he gets scared of some of the night sounds.

We don't know how Mercier got separated from the group. She may have been left behind when the females moved off to hunt at night (we have often seen females get up at dusk and just leave very young cubs totally undefended in the open). She must have spent hours calling for her pride mates. At seven months old she was still sucking a bit from Asti, one of the most tolerant females in the Santawani pride and she would have had no idea how to kill for herself. During those two and a half weeks she would have been forced to fend for herself and she might have scavenged or killed small animals.

It is also possible that Mercier joined up with some other females. This is not as strange as it sounds for we once saw a cub that belonged to the Gomoti pride join up with the Santawani pride. We nicknamed this cub the 'insect' as she was so tiny. She belonged to a young Gomoti female who had been in the Santawani territory for several days with the rest of the Gomoti pride. They must have left the 'insect' behind and Mum was astonished to find her a few days later with Santawani females Amarula and Sancerre and their nine cubs. This is an example of how vital IDs are, as Mum knew the 'insect' by her whisker pattern and nose colour. We couldn't believe that the pride had adopted her, the older cubs accepted her so well even though she was tiny. The females were very kind to her but as they had weaned their nine cubs quite early they had no milk for her. Sadly 'insect' didn't make it, but that adoption was an incredible thing to see.

When Mercier found her pride again she was very thin and bony and we watched her anxiously for weeks until she got strong again. For months all was well and the cubs grew more and more robust and became increasingly curious. Everything was fine until almost a year later when something terrible happened.

One January afternoon Mum and Pieter went out to find the lions by themselves. We stayed in camp with Emily, who had come home to spend Christmas with us. After a few hours Mum radioed through that they had found the Santawani pride, which had been missing for three weeks. The pride looked like it had been attacked; two cubs had been badly mutilated and one of them was Mercier. The skin on her throat had almost been ripped off and there was only raw flesh and sinew holding it together. The adults looked fine but eight of the nine smaller cubs were missing and some of the ten surviving cubs were appallingly wounded. We were horrified and waited by the radio for more news, as Mum and Pieter tried to identify the remaining cubs.

They had been out for hours and it was getting dark but still we had heard nothing. By nine o'clock we were getting worried. Our car in camp had something wrong with it and wasn't safe to drive at night in case it broke down. At ten o'clock we all decided to go to Corrie and Anne at Gomoti Camp and ask for help. We agreed it would be silly to go out to search for them in the dark, as we wouldn't be able to follow their tracks through the woods.

All of us, with Sophie, looking
at the video footage of the
wounded Santawani pride.

At six the next morning Corrie, Travers and Sophie (one of the students in camp) formed a search party, leaving Emily, Gus and me with Oakley. In the night Oakley had been crying and holding on to Emily saying 'Mummy's dead'. He and Emily had a big cry together but I knew things would turn out fine. After three hours of searching they found Mum and Pieter's footprints on the road, and a short time later, much to their relief, saw them walking towards camp.

What had happened was simple. Their battery had died while they were with the lions and they couldn't start the car or use the radio. The poor things had had to spend the night in the small cab of the Land Rover in a rain-storm with no

food. They knew we would all be desperately worried and therefore they started to walk home at first light. At one point a male lion roared right beside them but they never saw him. They had to walk five miles before they were picked up. Those of us in camp had kept ourselves busy by making a huge breakfast. At ten o'clock we heard a car and ran to see if it was them. We were worried when we saw only Corrie's car drive into camp, but then we all burst into joy when Mum and Pieter tumbled out of the car into our arms.

Over breakfast they told us about the lions. When Mum said that Pieter had cried when he saw them, we knew how bad it was. I was curious to see them

although Mum had warned us that it would be very distressing. That afternoon she took Emily and me to find the cubs. We left Oakley behind in camp with the others because Mum felt it was too much for him to take on.

The lions hadn't moved far from where they had been the night before and when I saw them I couldn't believe my eyes, it was gruesome. I said to myself, 'they are definitely going to die,' and I couldn't bear to watch as they licked each other's raw wounds. Mercier was the most wounded and lay on her bad side looking forlorn. I have seen lots of adult lions with very bad wounds and they all recovered. Their bodies are strong and can fight infection but we couldn't believe that such little lions could cope.

Over the next weeks we could see them treating each other's wounds by licking them and gradually we could see the wounds getting drier and start to close up. Months went by and everyone was more confident about their chances of survival. We started to hope. Mercier's head was tilting to one side as the skin stretched over her wound, which was healing fast. This made her look adorable and her little sideways head makes her the easiest lion to identify. Miraculously they all survived and are growing up even stronger than they might have been. This challenge may have made their bodies more immune to infection and sickness. It also showed us that we should never interfere with lion immune systems by treating their wounds, because if we had they would have had less of a chance of surviving. This was, and is, very hard because we love these lions dearly and we hate to see them in pain. We would help them if they were caught in a man-made trap or wounded by a man-made thing, but if they get wounded or sick naturally we leave them alone to fight their own battles. They do very well without our help.

Mercier months later, healed and doing well.

CHAPTER FOUR **COPING WITH PROBLEMS**

MEETING CHALLENGES

TRAVERS

LIFE IN THE BUSH is unpredictable and it has become clear to us that there are profound differences between living in the bush and merely visiting it. The challenges that life in camp has presented have been different for all of us. And while at times they have seemed overwhelming, because of our isolation, we have had to deal with them by working together as a team. Recently a raging bush fire threatened our camp. For three days we fought to put it out by beating it with spades and by burning the ground in front of the flames. All of us, including Oakley who was wearing his red fireman's hat, took an equal part; no one flagged as we all felt the same urgent need, not only to defend our camp, but also to stop the fire engulfing the plains and the forests.

In May 2000 I faced other challenges that I had never encountered before, and in doing so came to realise that if I couldn't do something I had to find a way to overcome that and meet the problem head on.

We had a lot to achieve in a short time. Three vets were coming from America to sample the lions. Our friend Jeff Gush, who is a safari operator, was to come out from Maun with the vets to set up a camp for them, to make sure everything ran smoothly and to guide them around the bush. The vets' task was to check the study lions for disease, as it is vitally important that the lions are sampled regularly. Some of the lions are FIV positive (feline immunodeficiency virus) and we need to monitor how this disease affects individuals and how it spreads throughout a pride. The vets had only three weeks to collect blood samples from the study lions, and we knew that this time scale meant that we would have to work non-stop under difficult conditions. At this time of year the game was very scattered because the rains had only just abated. There was an abundance of waterholes spread across the open plains and hidden in the thick forests. As a result the prey animals and our study lions were dispersed far and wide. We decided both cars had to go out tracking every morning, not always the easiest thing to manage, as they often need running repairs.

At the same time Pieter's book *Prides: The Lions of Moremi*, had recently been released in South Africa and was going to be launched by the publishers. They wanted to publicise the book by inviting the media, including three film crews, to our home to get an idea of life in a research camp. While we were excited about the book being published, the launch was a formidable prospect, as we knew the camp would be full, what with three vets, sixteen journalists and three cameramen. Luckily the publishers had arranged for the journalists to stay at Gomoti Camp, the tourist camp just down the road. We were going to have to shuffle a lot of people around if we were going to keep everybody happy. We had just finished a thirteen-week term and were well prepared for a working holiday but none of us could have guessed the worry that lay ahead.

A couple of days before the vets' arrival Pieter declared that he wasn't feeling very well and he was going to bed. Pieter doesn't get sick often but when he does, he gets *very* sick, and it's an absolute nightmare to treat him because he wants to be in complete control and will not listen to any advice. Also, like Nero, he demands a constant supply of grapes and cooling drinks. That night he was very sick, and shivers and shakes accompanied his raging fever. Mum knew instantly it was malaria because she had treated Angus and me; however, Pieter refused to believe it, as he had lived in Africa for fifteen years and had never contracted it before. The next morning Mum tested him with our home-testing malaria kit. This involves drawing a minute amount of blood with a pin and mixing it with several chemical agents that detect the presence of antibodies to the parasite. It is a very simple test but not all negative results are reliable. Pieter tested negative, which only fuelled his belief that he only had a bad dose of flu.

Both Mum and Angus had recently done an intensive medical course (which

BDF plain looking lush and green after heavy rains.

Angus writes about in Chapter 5), so there was a well-equipped medical kit in camp, which is extremely important as we live so far from Maun. Mum quickly pulled out the quinine from the kit. This is a very effective but toxic anti-malarial drug (made from the bark of a tree) and Pieter was reluctant to take it unless it was absolutely necessary. At this stage Pieter was still his usual articulate self and Mum could do nothing to persuade him. So with a heavy heart she left for town to meet the vets and introduce them to the Botswana Wildlife Department. This was an important meeting, for we work at the invitation of the Wildlife Department and they must be informed about all our work and collaborations with others. At times like these the responsibilities of the project and being a guest in someone else's country have to take precedence. Mum took Angus, Maisie and Oaks into town with her so that camp would be quiet for Pieter. This meant that I was left in charge together with Kate Evans (a student on the project, who has become a close family friend – Maisie will talk more about her later) and her English friend Peter Williams. Peter had only just arrived and was thrown into the deep end of our hectic family life.

By lunchtime Pieter's fever had risen alarmingly to 38.5 degrees and within an hour it had rocketed upwards to the dangerous level of 40.2 degrees. The fever was caused by the malaria parasites being released from thousands of red blood cells simultaneously. We knew that we shouldn't allow his temperature to go above 41 degrees, as there was a risk that he might have a seizure. Ironically he was feeling very cold and was dressed warmly, as well as being wrapped up in layers of blankets. As we tried to peel back the layers he became belligerent and called us terrorists, butchers and some other names I cannot write in this book. I could see that Pieter was scared but he refused to admit it. We finally succeeded in cooling him down by putting a damp sheet on top of him and taking off most of his clothes. We asked if he was peeing a lot because we were afraid he was becoming dehydrated but he replied that he was pissing like a racehorse (we later discovered this was not true, another example of his denial that he was very seriously ill). During all the blanket pulling and cooling down Mum was shouting down the radio telling us to give him quinine but he still refused. It was a horrible situation to be in: Mum was screaming, Pieter was trying to scream, Kate was frantic and I was in the middle of it.

Meanwhile, back in town, Maisie, who can trip over a twig, had sprained her ankle. This meant a trip to the hospital and more delays. To compound disaster, just as they were about to leave town, the car broke down badly. As a result Mum had to spend the night in town and get the car fixed first thing in the morning. She must have felt extremely frustrated.

Pieter was still refusing to believe he had malaria even though he was getting sicker and sicker. It can be very dangerous to delay taking the medication as the parasites build up unchecked and it becomes much more difficult to fight the illness. We tested him once more but frustratingly it again came out negative; Pieter sweated it out through the night while we slept deeply, exhausted.

Everyone was frantic with worry and to this day none of us know why Pieter didn't want to believe he had the dangerous illness. Perhaps the fear of taking the quinine, a toxic drug, which can often make you feel sicker than having malaria, made him delay as long as possible.

Mum got back that evening and tested him for the third time. At last a positive result came up. Surely he would believe us now, but no, Pieter still said that it was *not* malaria. Mum radioed the Scottish nurse Allison Brown. 'Of course the test is right!' Allison yelled. 'Tell him to stop being so stubborn and take the medication right now!' So, very grudgingly and at long last, Pieter started the seven-day course of quinine.

The drug causes your ears to ring continuously, gives you pins and needles, and also makes you feel very nauseous. Poor Pieter has a horror of puking so he got more and more miserable. He had a high fever all through the day and Mum kept taking his temperature every twenty minutes. We plastered him with wet cloths and kept peeling back the blankets but he would grip on to them so tightly that his knuckles went white. All the while he was singing all sorts of songs including the whole of *Jesus Christ Superstar*, this made us laugh a lot but we were also desperately worried as he was obviously delirious.

Suddenly things started to go really badly, he could not even keep water down, and he was getting more and more dehydrated. By the next day his skin had turned pale yellow and his pee was almost black. He was getting weaker and weaker. It scared me a lot to see him like that. Mum knew he had to have an IV drip to try and rehydrate him. She was just about to put it up when, much to her relief, Jeff Gush arrived. He immediately helped her by putting up the drip. We all knew Pieter should be in hospital but he was afraid of going to Maun, as he knew what the hospital was like. He promised faithfully he would keep drinking and begged to be allowed to stay in his own bed.

As usual we had a vehicle crisis. The white car's radiator had acquired a hole and so Kate and I had to go to town to pick up a new radiator. We also needed to get some more valoid for Pieter, a drug that helps to prevent vomiting and nausea. We arrived in town and started to do the usual stuff, shopping for fresh food, picking up the gas bottles, filling fuel cans and collecting the precious mail. Everything was going well and we planned to be back in camp by late afternoon, but we couldn't have been more wrong. At the garage a very over-stretched foreman showed us briefly how to put in the radiator once we were back in camp, impressing upon us the importance of a minute rubber seal; on no account was this critical object to be lost. We listened intently and prayed we would remember all the relevant details. As we were walking out the door Sue Bateman, who runs the garage with her husband Rod, came up to us looking very concerned and asked us if Pieter was okay because she had heard some worrying news. She said that she had just heard over the open radio channel that he was being evacuated from camp by helicopter. Kate and I knew that Mum would only have called Med-rescue in an emergency and we were terrified.

I felt helpless, I didn't know where to turn, we couldn't talk to Mum so it was up to us to get everything sorted out in Maun. A wave of fear shot through me, I remembered that Pieter did not have any medical insurance and without this he would not be able to fly out of camp, so we ran around town getting things organised financially. I phoned great friends of Mum's in England and asked if they could cover the costs. Asking to borrow money from someone I didn't know very well was a nerve-wracking experience, but luckily they agreed instantly. We will never forget their kindness. Kate and I then went to the airport and anxiously awaited Pieter's arrival.

I was not in camp as he flew out and I will leave Oakley to tell you what happened there.

" We could hear the helicopter from far away, it was very noisy and it was getting closer and closer. It landed in Gomoti Camp, me and Peter Williams drived to the camp and drove the person over to our camp so that Allison could look at the very sick Pieter. I could have gone in the chopper but they didn't say that so I couldn't go. Then it flowed over to camp and it landed right next to the tent. I asked the pilot if I could look inside and he said yes. I pressed a button that would drop a bomb because it was a Botswana Defence Force helicopter but there was no bombs in. Inside the chopper there was a bed where Pieter could lie down. He got in the car and was drived to the helicopter and then hobbled into the helicopter with help from people. As it took off lots of sand went up into the air and into our eyes. Mummy went with Pieter as well so we were alone in camp with small Peter. I was very sad for Pieter but he was lucky to fly in the helicopter I wish I could have gone. "

It took fifteen minutes for the helicopter to fly to Maun. On arrival Pieter looked absolutely terrible but he managed to tell me that he thought that everyone was overreacting. He had to have two men help him into a car five metres away but he was still convinced that it was all just nonsense. He was rushed to Maun hospital by car, where we fought to see a very busy and stressed-out doctor. Pieter was told that he had severe dehydration and his body could not cope with the malaria. He was also having trouble keeping the quinine down, so this meant that the malaria was blooming inside him. He was told he was going to need at least three days attached to an IV. Pieter was booked into the last private room left in the hospital. It turned out to be not so private.

We wheeled Pieter past the open tents where very sick patients were lying on the ground, past the packed wards full of bemused people visiting their families, past the labour room that was right by the loos, along the corridors that were lined with mattresses and into his tiny room that had just two beds and a few pieces of old furniture. Within seconds he was asleep, oblivious to the noise of the screaming babies next door. The deafness caused by the quinine was protecting him from the outside world and he lay in a stupor fighting the parasite with all his might.

The hospital was so full because it was the only one in the region. The Ministry of Health runs the hospital so it is almost free of charge. It is, however, often under-

staffed. AIDS and malaria patients stretch the resources of the hospital almost to breaking point. African people get paid very meagre salaries so they cannot afford mosquito nets, insect repellent and other forms of protection against this killer insect. When they do contract malaria the medication is quite expensive so when they finally go to hospital they are extremely sick. Even the hospital provides no mosquito nets, so if you are admitted without malaria there is a good chance you will contract it in the hospital itself. Malaria need not be the killer disease it is, if only people could be treated sooner and were able to afford better precautions.

That night Mum slept on the floor by Pieter's bed listening to his every breath. The next morning Pieter was looking a bit better and was finally keeping water down but he was still on a drip. The following morning Kate and I went to do a few errands in town.

A few errands turned out to be a lot of errands and before we knew it, it was starting to get dark. We left Mum and Pieter at the hospital; sensibly the doctor had said he must spend one more night but could leave the following morning. Mum and Kate agreed that Kate would collect them with the white car. That way we could put down the seats and make a bed for Pieter in the back. As Kate and I drove back we almost passed out with exhaustion but then to our horror we remembered that the white car's radiator was still broken.

We got back to a very worried little camp. We reassured everyone and had a quick supper before we tackled the radiator problem. I was desperate to make sure Kate was on time in the morning and to get Pieter safely home. I had helped Pieter put a radiator into a Toyota before and that was quite easy, but the Land Rover turned out to be different. An hour later, struggling by torch light, covered in sand and oil, we were lying beneath the car untightening the last bolts with rapidly numbing fingers, when I dropped the vital rubber seal that we knew we should not lose, and helplessly watched it vanish into the deep sand. At this point Kate nearly burst into tears. I tried to reassure her that all was well and we could make a plan; as I spoke I picked up the bowl filled with all the nuts and bolts we had already removed to show her how well we had done. In my enthusiasm I forgot my oily fingers, and moments later the sand devoured our good night's work. After half an hour, having *sieved* through the sand, we picked up the last bolt and decided to call it a night.

In the calm light of day the whole operation was completed comparatively quickly, and we wondered why we hadn't waited until the morning in the first place. A few hours later, Pieter and Mum were home again, much to our relief, and things went back to normal. Pieter was still very weak and wan, but he started to build up his strength bit by bit. He sat in the sun outside his tent soaking up the warmth and trying to regain some colour as the book launch was only two days away.

The journalists arrived with our good friends Chris and Maggi Harvey. Chris conceived *Prides* with Pieter and took the photographs. That night Pieter and Mum joined them for supper but came back early because the whole thing exhausted Pieter.

The next morning I was woken up by the sound of impalas dashing through camp, barking their alarm calls. I lay in bed listening intently when I heard the rasping sound of an impala taking its last breath. I unzipped my tent just as the sun was peeking over the horizon and saw three cheetahs eating a baby impala; they had killed it right next to my bedroom. This isn't an everyday occurrence. Mum decided that it would be a brilliant opportunity for the film crew and sped off to collect them, still wearing her pyjamas. Oakley, as usual unable to miss a thing, climbed into the car with her in spite of the fact he was naked.

Surprisingly it took Mum some time to rouse the film crew and meanwhile the cheetahs were busily bolting their meal. When she finally arrived with the more alert members of the team, they were delighted by the shots provided and got stuck into the filming. However, a few minutes later their joy turned to irritation, as a fellow journalist bounced up the road, bleary eyed and oblivious, and scared the cheetahs off. He was clearly unaware of how shy these predators are, and we could only be grateful, for his sake, that the cheetahs weren't lions.

After the cheetah ordeal we had to make breakfast in front of the cameras and were asked 'What's it like living in the bush?' over and over again. The whole morning was a blur of cameras and reporters. When people come to see us they like to idealise our life. They don't want to hear about getting into damp sheets on a rainy night, digging a new loo when one has filled up, and vomiting at midnight with no running water or electricity. We couldn't move around camp without being asked to pose in the sun, look admiringly at Pieter's book, cook a pancake or patch an inner tube. Quite genuinely Angus and I had three tyres to fix, as the vets wanted to go tracking in the afternoon. At one point while I was being asked questions by four reporters, Mum and Maggi were asked by a cameraman to stand by the cooker and pretend to bake a cake, while Chris and Pieter did something manly. As you can imagine this was like a red rag to a bull, and Mum, with unusual restraint, suggested an alternative activity. Little did that cameraman know that his entire reproductive system was at that moment in dire jeopardy.

Luckily, that afternoon the lions needed to be found and I willingly volunteered to help the vets. I left camp with my head still reeling from the morning's activities and relished the peace of the bush. Following me were some extremely happy vets who were thrilled to have finally started work.

The three vets were called Mike, Mike and Asa (so that you don't get confused, we called them big Mike and little Mike). Big Mike is colossal and looks like a bear but has a heart of gold once you get to know him. Little Mike is, well, small. He is a pathologist and was beside himself with excitement that he would be working with *live* wild lions. And then there was Asa, blonde, Swedish and looking about eighteen. Peter Williams thought he had died and gone to heaven and followed her around trying to satisfy her every wish.

My job was to locate the lions and then radio through to camp so that Mum could come out and identify the lions that needed sampling. We feel very protective of the study lions and we never let anyone work with them unless they are with one of us. It takes years to build up trust with an animal and one stupid mistake can undo months of patience and care. We were all very touched by the Mikes' obvious love of the animals and they respected our concern.

To look at diseases the lions may have been in contact with, the vets had to

Cheetah: the shyest of all predators.

take blood samples, which obviously required the lions to be anaesthetised. This has to be done in a calm environment so that the animal is kept relaxed. No one is allowed to make unnecessary movements and all voices are kept down to a quiet whisper. When a lion is anaesthetised it is extremely vulnerable to other predators, so there was always a person on look out for any other lions and at least two vehicles formed a protective shield around the animal.

Once the lion was asleep they checked for external parasites like mites and ticks, looked at the condition of the teeth to see how old the lion was, took body measurements and then collected the blood samples that were later processed in America. When all the work was completed everyone backed away and left the lion to recover in peace, watching from a distance until it was back on its feet and able to protect itself. You may be wondering whether this whole process is necessary. No one likes immobilising wild animals but it is very important to have an understanding of what diseases lions are in contact with so that we can protect them better and make sure that the population remains healthy.

As I have said many of the study lions are FIV positive; indeed we have now discovered that 90% of the study lions are infected. This high rate of infection has caused Mum and Pieter to be very concerned. FIV is the cat equivalent to HIV which leads to AIDS. Up until now is has been thought that FIV among lions was not as deadly as HIV among humans but attitudes are changing. FIV is deadly to domestic cats and captive lions have been seen to suffer negative effects four years after infection; resulting in a rapid decline in their overall health, wasting and finally death.

We have been following known positive lions for four years, and while some seem perfectly healthy, others have rapidly wasted as they get older. Perhaps more worryingly Mum and Pieter have noticed that some of the younger females, who are FIV positive, are not reproducing successfully. As yet it is too early to say if this is due to FIV but it is now an urgent focus of their research.

Pieter was overjoyed to be back in the field again and though he was still thin, he looked remarkably well for a man who had almost died. Looking after Pieter when he was that sick made me scared, but at the time I just got on with the practical issues at hand and didn't let myself think about losing him. It was later that I realised how close we'd come. I cannot imagine what life would be without him; I have learned to love him and need him.

Not all the challenges at that time were generated by our life in the bush. Three months after the vets' visit, my friend Sebastian Kohler encouraged Angus, me and our friends to form an eclectic team that would play against the Namibians in the Coastal Pirates Roller Hockey Tournament 2000.

Soon our little group was training ferociously twice a week. This was no

Pieter measuring Shiraz's canine. When a lion is anaesthetised no one is allowed to make unnecessary movements and all voices are kept down to a quiet whisper.

mean feat because it meant a two-hour drive for Angus and I from the Lion Research Camp. Even for those living in town, transport was a big problem. Our friends the two Boddington brothers, Adrian and Matthew, and Ross Cunningham had to hitch-hike, walk or take a taxi to the Thamalakane River, which they then had to cross by boat, and walk still further to get to practice.

Sandy who built the rink for the Maun community is a great believer in self-motivation and while the court was made freely available to us we had to coach ourselves. After five months of hard training Sandy showed his faith in us by entering our team, the Mukwa Leafs Eighteen and Under, in the Namibian tournament that was to be held at Swakopmund, a small town on the coast of the Atlantic, where we dared to go swimming in the freezing waters. We were all excited as well as daunted by the prospect of playing in an international tourna-

ment. We took a look at ourselves and realised our equipment was far from adequate; we needed gloves, new sticks and lots more padding. Sandy held the annual Tequila Cup Tournament to raise funds for the equipment. The whole town rallied and the day of the Tequila Cup was filled with laughter. The adults cheered the younger children's teams, the Power Rangers and the Barbies, all afternoon. As night fell the three Mukwa Leaf teams entered for the Namibian tournament took to the rink. Our team, the Ladies team and the Masters played friendly matches all evening, cheered on by an increasingly merry crowd; it's not called the Tequila Cup for nothing!

One week before the tournament our tension was mounting. Would our small

Angus (aged 10) on goal! Sandy's rollerblading rink in the early days.

team survive up against the more experienced Namibians? To our delight a new German boy called Florian Bendson had just arrived in Maun, with his cousin Jan. They were both good roller hockey players, and we eagerly welcomed them into the team. After our last training session we realised none of us had any matching uniforms. So the evening before we left for Swakopmund, we painted cheap t-shirts with fabric paints and glued pieces of bed matting together to act as protection for our hips and thighs. Meanwhile Sebastian's parents Reiner and Birgit Kohler busily loaded their car in preparation for the long-haul, night drive to Namibia.

Our home-made uniforms had looked fine in Maun, but two days later, standing in the changing room at Swakopmund, we all had second thoughts. We felt ridiculous beside the immaculately turned out, heavily sponsored (and padded.) Namibian teams. They looked us up and down and couldn't help giggling. Ten minutes later, with our stomachs in a knot and our hands trembling, we bladed on to the massive indoor rink. It was twice the size of our little rink in Maun that now seemed so far away, and the surface didn't have a crack in sight. The stands were packed with noisy spectators and lights blazed down upon us. We warmed up under the gaze of hundreds of pairs of eyes, desperately hoping we wouldn't embarrass ourselves too much. The notion of winning seemed a Herculean task.

As the first whistle blew all our nerves were blown away and, inspired by the atmosphere, we started to play harder than we had ever played before. Sandy frantically substituted players and shouted instructions from the sidelines. As the half-time whistle blew we were all on an adrenaline rush. We were winning 4-0. Sandy told us to calm down and continue to play as well as we had done in the first half, but not to get too confident. We decided just to have fun and enjoyed playing together as we did at home. Soon the game was over and we had *won* 7-1. Sandy looked more excited than any of us, and told us to get some rest as the next game was in an hour. We all went outside, lay on a football field and ate bananas, unable to grasp the fact we had actually won our first game in our first tournament.

As we were preparing for our next game someone came up to us and warned us that the team we were playing, the Kamikazis, were pretty rough, and we might get knocked about a bit. We hurriedly stuffed some bed matting down our shorts and taped it firmly into place with Sellotape. With a little bit of padding and some residue of confidence left over from our recent win, we bladed on to the court to meet our opponents. As the whistle blew we skated fast and hard, we were thrown around a bit as they body-checked us against the boards; as predicted it was a rough and challenging first half but miraculously we came out of it equally, the score was 2-2.

During half time Sandy urged us on and uncharacteristically told us to play rougher. The second half was even faster and more frantic, but we came out of it very well, the final score was 5-2. We had won again. As you can imagine none of us got much sleep that night, as we were all on a high and looking forward to the next day.

We had made it to the final; none of us could believe it. Nerves tore through our bodies and the Coastal Pirates flattened us, beating us 7-1. But our blood is up and we are all determined to go back next year and *win*. When we got home to camp Oaks wanted the stories of the matches told again and again, and he is now determined to bring his own team to Namibia this year. Knowing him, he'll probably do it.

The challenges that I dealt with during the first half of 2000 were clearly defined and easy to see. Not all problems are that straightforward; during this time Maisie had her own challenges that were not so obvious to everyone in camp.

GIRLS IN THE BUSH
MAISIE

THE BUSH IS A BOY'S WORLD and we girls try to make the best of it. I don't mind all the tough things we have to do like changing tyres, collecting water and getting unstuck from huge amounts of mud but it's nice to do something girlie once in a while. One weekend my best friend Lena came and stayed in camp. I have known Lena for five years now and during those years we have grown close: we are very alike. She is a calm person, who makes me laugh. She has a benign and welcoming family. I usually go and stay with Lena, but when she comes to our camp my Mum gives her the same 'our home is your home' welcome.

Lena and I talked for hours in my tent until the light started to fade then

Mum asked if we wanted to go on a 'Girlie Game Drive' with her and Kate Evans, who I'll talk about later. It was a balmy night; the air was still and warm. We decided to stop at Jackal Pan, one of our favourite waterholes, to see what animals came to drink. Lena and I climbed on to the roof of the car and lay on a mattress, looking up at the sky. There was only a sliver of moon and the sky was saturated with stars. I can remember a hyena coming to drink and a couple of elephants wallowing peacefully in the pan. We heard ducks taking off from the water and some jackals yowling in the distance. The fresh elephant dung smelt like wet grass and a soft breeze wafted the smell over the roof of the car. After a while we moved on, and Lena and I stayed on the roof.

We drove slowly along the road, using a spotlight plugged into the cigarette lighter to shine on the plains around us. Lena and I were talking and not alert to the reflection caused by wild animals' eyes when Mum cried, 'Get in the car!' We looked around and saw three sub-adult male lions very close to us. We scrambled through the windows and jumped into the back seat. I noticed the lions were on a kill but could not work out what it was. I thought it was the stomach of something but there was no blood; then suddenly I figured it out, it was a pangolin, the rarest mammal in Africa. I haven't seen anything that looks like a pangolin so it's hard to describe. They are covered in scales and when they are frightened they curl up into a ball, like a hedgehog. Pangolins have very sweet, soothing, pointed

little faces, and the colour of their body is a soft grey with splashes of brown in some parts. They move very slowly and calmly. They eat termites and ants and no one knows when they evolved, but they look millions of years old. The lions played with the pangolin like a soccer ball for a while but eventually got bored. They could not break through its tough scales, and walked off in disgust. We watched mesmerised as the pangolin slowly uncurled itself.

Mum got out of the car very quietly, gently lifted the pangolin and carefully placed it on to a pillow on my lap. It was a thrill to hold such a rare and primitive

Kate Evans and Oakley relaxing by the river. Kate is a very special person to us all.

animal. I wonder what they do all the time by themselves. I haven't heard of any people who research them, but I know there must be some because who wouldn't want to research something as incredible as that? I passed the pillow and the pangolin to Lena so she could feel how wonderful it was. We left it in peace, and after watching it move slowly off across the plain we drove home looking forward to telling everyone our news. I could see Kate had been deeply moved by this extraordinary experience.

I must tell you about Kate Evans, as she is a very special person to me. She joined the project in August 1999 and helped it by working on parasites found in lion faeces. Ever since she arrived she has felt like a sister to me. I found it hard when Emily left home, but now whenever I miss her I go and talk to Kate. Even though she is thirteen years older than I am she is very easy to talk to. She is a warm, gentle person and has a strong heart. She arrived with Sophie Greatwood, her best friend. Sadly Sophie only stayed a few months and left to do another job. This was hard for Kate as she was in a new place and felt that Sophie was the only one she could go to with her problems or when she was feeling down. Kate has always felt like part of the family to me but I think it took her a bit longer to feel comfortable with that.

She was born in Taunton, Somerset, and then moved to Turkey, Pakistan and later Finland. Tragically, when she was only twelve, her much loved mother died. After that she lived with her father and brother and they are a very close family. She went to university and later travelled and worked all over Southern Africa before she arrived in Botswana to research hippos. Mum met her by accident one day when Kate was hitching for a lift out of Botswana after her work with the hippos was over. Mum liked her immediately and invited her to join us. We have always been careful to treat the lions with respect and we knew that Kate would do the same, as she loves animals.

Kate and I would always help each other with our problems. Once, Kate had had a particularly rough day: by accident she had broken some equipment and Mum and Pieter had been furious with her. So, to cheer her up, I went with her to have hot chocolate with the lions. We threw the thermos into the car, and went to poop the females that she had found earlier. We sat for hours waiting for the lions to 'do their stuff', quietly chatting and drinking our comfort drink. After a while they got up from their day's rest and we worked hard identifying each squatting female. Once they had moved off Kate got out to collect the steaming samples. On the way home we stopped off at a pan to look at all of the different kinds of ducks and geese while the sun was setting. Fortunately we had

arrived at a perfect time. A pack of beautiful Wild Dogs came to drink at the pan. 'This has made my day a whole lot better,' said

Our beautiful stepsisters, Marieke, Frieda and Philippa on a night time picnic.

Kate, and we drove home to leave the dogs in peace. Kate has helped me through some complicated times, such as the time when our new stepsisters were introduced in to our family.

In August 1999 there was a big change in camp that was exciting but also proved to be difficult. As Angus has already mentioned, Pieter has three daughters who live in America with their mother, Lucy. The two eldest, Philippa and Frieda, decided to come and visit us for the summer, for the first time. We were very anxious about meeting them, as we didn't know whether they would like us or not. We also wondered how they would fit into this environment, coming from America. But we needn't have worried as they were brought up in Kenya and knew Africa well.

It was in Kenya that something very sad happened to Philippa when she was eight months old. The malaria was bad at that time and her mother was on medicine to stop her getting it. By mistake Philippa got hold of some pills and took an overdose. Her Nanny found her unconscious on the floor. She was rushed to hospital, but she suffered a lack of oxygen and her brain was slightly damaged. Pieter wasn't very clear about how bad the damage was, so we didn't know how we would have to treat her when she came. But we were excited about meeting them and counted the days until they would arrive. Pieter flew to Johannesburg to pick up his girls and spend a night with them at a hotel. It must have been hard for them to know that other kids were living with their Dad, and I thought it was a good idea for them to have some 'Dad Time' alone before meeting all of us.

Angus, Travers and I waited for fifteen minutes at the airport, it seemed like hours. We were all nervous because Pieter and Mum weren't there and it was weird meeting our stepsisters for the first time. When we saw Pieter coming down the steps with his daughters, they looked nervous too, and Philippa later told me that her knees were shaking she was so apprehensive. Finally they were there and Pieter introduced us. We were all very shy but I could see at a glance that they were very nice. Philippa had a permanent smile on her face and we could see that she was as excited as we were. She didn't seem at all disabled; all she had was a slightly wobbly walk. Frieda was very pretty but looked more serious; apparently she was worried about missing some school back home in the States, but I think she was afraid of being part of a new family.

Pieter took us to have lunch at a fast food joint called Steers. It was a strange meal because no one spoke. Pieter asked simple questions like, 'How was your flight to Jo'berg?' and 'How was the food?'. We ate our lunch in total silence until Pieter suddenly got up and said, 'I have to go and get something. I'll be back.' We were all left looking at each other and when we caught each other's eyes we looked away. Travers and I nearly burst into hysterics when our eyes met. It was all so humiliating. It was Frieda who finally broke the silence by saying, 'Do you want to look at a photo of Marieke?' We all said, 'Sure,' and she pulled out a picture of their beautiful younger sister. I thought she looked really nice and couldn't wait to meet her. This broke the ice and we started to talk about what music we liked and a little about America.

The drive back to camp was a little tense and I found this irritating because all I wanted to do was talk, but I didn't want to open my mouth in case I made a fool of myself, since Travers was doing well enough at this himself. He couldn't stop talking about his weekend and what they all did. No one seemed in the least interested and therefore by the time we hit the buffalo fence he shut up. Oh no, I thought, another *hour* of this frustration before we get home. Even the animals let us down, for we saw no game on the entire journey. Poor Pieter must have been feeling as desperate as we all were because he stopped the car to pick a leaf from a mopane tree. 'Look,' he said, 'this is green and shaped like a butterfly, elephants eat them.' It was a tragic attempt to break the silence. Mum had stayed in camp to prepare for their arrival. We were all hugely relieved when her jolly voice broke in over the radio. 'Land Rover One, Land Rover One, come in please.' She had called to see how we all were and to talk to the girls. We could hear her excitement and she chatted for ages. Finally we arrived in camp and Philippa will tell you how she felt.

" It had been strange at the airport to see my dad with three unknown kids. But I had the feeling I would get to know them like people I had known all my life. I was silent in the car because I was very tired from all the planes we had been on. I was just so happy to see my dad and relieved I didn't have to take a plane for some time. The camp looked cosy and all lit up by candles; Frieda and I got two big warm welcoming hugs from Kate and Oakley. He couldn't stop talking and to this day he still hasn't!

I felt strange meeting these new people. Since my dad hadn't told us very much, I didn't know what to expect. I had been to camps in Kenya but they were all tourist camps, I had never been to a family camp. It felt like a home because we had to do things ourselves, it had used furniture, not all polished tables and side plates. There were books and toys and teddies on the sofa. Over supper everyone was talking and Kate was telling us how everyone was looking forward to meeting us, and how to say hello in Setswana, 'Dumela'. She told us about the switch on Oakley's back that would supposedly stop him from making a huge cacophony at the dinner table. We ate eggplant bake and vegetarian sausages, I liked it but wasn't sure about the vegetarian sausages.

We were very tired and my dad drove us to our tent with our suitcases. At the dinner table Kate had told us if we needed anything in the night just to call out as her tent was very close by. She told us she had had six kids and was used to being woken on a regular basis. She came to kiss us good night with our dad and warned us if we needed to pee in the night not to wander about the camp but to go outside our tent. Maisie, Frieda and I got ready for bed and lay in bed chatting for a while about movies and nonsense. I felt uneasy about sleeping in a tent, when I hadn't for five years. Frieda got to sleep okay but I think she was feeling the same way. In the middle of the night I woke up because I heard an elephant crashing about and I couldn't get back to sleep. I didn't call Kate, I don't know why. I called Frieda a couple of times but she was sound asleep. After a while I dozed off. Now I can sleep through pretty much anything as I have got used to the bush again.

In the morning daddy came to see how we were and showed us around the camp. I hadn't thought the camp would be as big as it was, and I felt good about being in the bush again. After having toast and whatnot we went out with our dad to see the lions. I remember we took gingernut biscuits for a snack. Daddy tracked at the first tracking mound and got a signal for Amarula and Sancerre. I was very excited we were about to see daddy's lions, but I was pretty surprised at how tough the going was. Frieda somehow spotted the lions through a triangle of trees. As we drove up I could see tiny cubs and my dad introduced us to part of the Santawani pride. A female called Cliquot was with them; in September '99, to our great distress, we found her carcass on the sand road leading to Maun. I was devastated because she was becoming my favourite lion.

Over the next few days we all got to know each other better and felt comfortable enough to make jokes, laugh and have fun together. **"**

Death

Death is a common thing
I have known two deaths
of lions whom I have loved.
One was said to be a fight and
the other I do not know,
like people do not know how
the wind blows.
Driving back from town one
day we saw the carcass and on
the ground it lay.
We checked the whisker pattern
it was her, Cliquot, alright
We drove home in the
Moonlight and shed our tears.

by Philippa

When we went back to our usual home school, Philippa joined our class with Mum. Pieter taught Frieda separately as she had so much work to complete for her school. School and lions filled up the next few weeks until it was nearly time for the girls to return to America. At this point Philippa started to have some doubts about going back to school in the States. There were forty students in her class and when she didn't understand something she was shy about asking, and this brought her down. The damage to her brain meant that everything was that much harder for her; for example she didn't learn to walk until she was two. At Mum's school she gained confidence because it was one-on-one teaching and Philippa felt safe to ask questions in front of us.

During the next trip to town Flip rang her mum, Lucy, to ask if she could stay to do school with us. Lucy said yes. I was very happy as it meant that I would have someone to work with in class and a friend in camp. So, Philippa would stay and we gave Frieda the best last week possible. She spent a lot of time alone with her dad and we had the idea to give her a surprise dinner on her last night before going back to America.

It took a lot of planning, as it is not easy to keep secrets in our camp. We sent her on a driving lesson with Pieter, who had strict instructions to keep her occupied practising hill starts until we gave him the signal over the radio that all was ready. Travers, lovingly known as the Fat Controller, was pointing fingers in all directions ordering people around. He told Philippa and me to go to our tent and get dressed up, while he and Gus drove to our secret pan and set up tables, chairs, the gas stove, candles and music. Meanwhile Mum was cooking one of Frieda's favourite meals, pizza, and crepe suzettes for pudding.

The scene was set and looked beautiful for Frieda's entrance. The candles were lit, and we played some cool music. We saw the lights of their car in the distance getting bigger and bigger, Frieda later told me she thought we were tourists camping illegally. She never guessed that the twinkling lights she saw were us until Oakley ran in front of the car; luckily she had learned how to do an emergency stop. When she saw the entire kitchen set up on the pan she burst into tears, 'Oh you guys, man, thank you so much'. Angus, with his usual insensitivity, did not notice that she was crying as he was stuffing his face with the snacks laid out on the table. After supper we danced for hours under the stars and played charades, and animal, vegetable, mineral, until the whole thing degenerated into hysterical giggles and we went home.

When Philippa arrived we set out on a new phase in our life. It was wonderful to have a stepsister but it was hard introducing someone new into our school, long term. She had not spent four years learning with Mum, and didn't understand our system. After some hiccups she just went with the flow and things got

easier but it was very difficult having her join our family and something happened that hurt me very much.

During the first week of school Mum was asking Flip all the questions and that was fine. But after a while it was quite annoying, as we wanted to show that we knew the answers as well as anyone else. I told Mum this and she apologised and explained that she had done it to see if Philippa was focused. From then on she asked everyone questions and things went back to normal, at school that is…

When Philippa first came to live with us Mum was giving her a lot of attention. I recognised that she wanted Flip to know that she was welcome into her unfamiliar stepfamily. It worked: she soon settled in and felt safe and confident, but I found all the attention she got from Mum quite hard. For instance, when Mum got back from a game drive the first thing she said was 'Where's Flip?' 'Mmmm, well she's on the sofa over there.' Mum was always asking me if she was okay and whether we had had any disagreements. I found it quite annoying constantly having to reassure her : 'No, no, she's fine you don't have to worry about her so much, I promise she's fine.'

Another problem was the cuddling. We have always been a very cuddly family but it seemed that Mum was only cuddling Flip and I had to *go to* Mum if I wanted a hug. I thought I was being too sensitive and overreacting so I kept it inside for a long, long time. I also didn't say anything to Mum because I thought I would hurt her feelings. I knew she loved me but I thought she was beginning to love Philippa more. Finally it was hurting so much that I told Mum. Things started to change and I felt much better. When, after three months, Philippa left to spend time in the States we all missed her badly but I was able to relax back into my relationship with Mum. Stepfamilies are actually more complicated than one imagines.

A few months later Flip came back to camp and I was very happy to see her, but soon I felt the dormant feelings erupt again. Now I really thought I was being stupid and over-sensitive and was afraid to tell Mum. I could see she was trying to be fair, like when she kissed me, she kissed Flip and vice versa. I kept my feelings inside again and didn't even tell Kate.

However, something happened at school that brought them to the surface. Philippa and I had been asked to translate a seventeenth-century poem by Robert Southey into modern-day language. It was an interesting poem called 'An Ode to a Pig While His Nose is Being Bored'. We worked on it separately and I finished first. When I showed it to Mum she was thrilled and said it was a very good piece of work. Later that afternoon when she had marked it she whispered into my ear, 'That work gets an A, Maisie.' I was very pleased but confused about why she had had to whisper the information. Anyway I was getting on with other work and when Philippa showed Mum her translation, Mum was full of praise. 'This is amazing work, this is by far the best work you have done recently, you should be proud of yourself.' I was bitterly hurt that my praise had not been given so publicly.

That night we were preparing to go on a game drive. While the boys were loading the car with drinks, biscuits and blankets Mum gave me a cuddle and started saying how much she loved me. That's when all my months' pain and hurt came out of my eyes. Mum held me close and we stayed behind alone and talked by candlelight; I told her everything. She totally understood my misery and said how sorry she was not to have seen it sooner. She said that nothing and no one could ever take my place in her heart.

Now settled, I could get through the day comfortably and school went back to normal. It wasn't as if Mum had a teacher's pet, as she treated us equally. Home school has its drawbacks: you don't have friends to work with and at the end of the day you don't have the thrill of the bell ringing and everyone screaming 'School's out', and jumping into the car to go home. But I love being taught by my mother because if I have a problem I can go to her with ease and if I don't understand something I can tell her without being embarrassed. In the best of all possible worlds I would love to go to regular school sometimes and have home school as well. Mum and I have found a compromise.

A year ago Lena and lots of my other friends left Maun to go to boarding school in South Africa, I was devastated and missed them terribly. Because I was so sad my friends had left, I was stupid enough not to make other friends and felt very lonely. Mum was really worried about me and said that I could take my holidays whenever Lena and the others came back to Maun. This is not as easy as it sounds, as Mum has to keep to Botswana term time for the boys' social life, American term time to incorporate Flip, and English holidays for our cousins and friends from home. It's great for me as South African schools have four short terms and lots of holidays. As I am writing this I am about to go to town and start a long holiday with Lena while the boys and Flip have three weeks to go. But the bad news is that I have got to go and do a test now…

HOME SCHOOL

ANGUS

WHEN WE LIVED IN ENGLAND, we all went to regular country schools. As Travers has told you, Emily was very happy at Chipping Camden Comprehensive, Travers was at a small, friendly school called Bruern Abbey that specialised in dyslexia and Maisie and I went to Blockley Primary just up the hill from Hollybush Cottage. In the morning our house was chaotic with four of us trying to grab breakfast and get ready. There was always last-minute reading to be done, lost homework to find, crumpled letters for school trips to sign, forgotten PE kits to find under my bed, pogs and football cards to stuff into our satchels to later swap at school, and usually a fight over the prize in the cornflakes packet. Even after all this Mum would have to turn back at the end of the drive to collect a forgotten lunch box.

I was very happy at school, had loads of friends, got along well with all the teachers and there weren't any problems with bullying. I am quite a social person and took part in most of the school activities, and really loved doing plays. Each evening after homework I would climb over the stile that led into our neighbours' garden to play football with our good friend Greg. Our school life was very normal and we could not imagine any other, so when Mum asked us if we wanted to move to Africa naturally one of our main questions was, 'What are we going to do about school?'

She told us that she had found a good school in Maun named Matshwane (this means 'honey badger' in Setswana). We thought that was a really weird name for a school and had hundreds of questions to ask: 'Will we be taught in English? What games do they play? What is the food like? Do they wear a uniform? Can the children speak English?' Mum was able to put our minds at rest over a few of these enquires but we were still worried. Moving schools was one thing, but moving to one on a whole new continent was incredible. I remember my teacher asking me to show my class where we were going to live, and I could only point vaguely at a map of Southern Africa and reply, 'I'm not quite sure, but I think it's around here'. Saying goodbye to my school friends was surprisingly easy, because I had no idea it would be so long before I would see them again. I thought the move was more like a big holiday, none of it seemed real to me. Even our first few weeks in Africa just seemed like an adventure; it was only on my first day of school that it dawned on me that the move was for real.

Mum and Oakley drove Travers, Maisie and me to school. We were unusually silent and nervously clutched our new water bottles and lunch boxes. Matshwane was astonishingly different to Blockley. The ground was all bare sand, and the buildings were made out of whitewashed concrete. 'Where's the football pitch?' I asked. I was used to playing on a strip of lush green grass and was disappointed to be shown a big dust-bowl with some goal posts at either end. Also, the classrooms were in separate buildings, and instead of a huge colourful assembly hall, the students gathered each morning under a corrugated roof and sat on a concrete floor. Poor Maisie felt very out of place that first morning because, to her mortification, she was forced to wear her old Blockley uniform. The supplies of uniforms in Maun had run out and the headmistress had asked for her to be dressed in the closest approximation. She didn't have any school socks either, so she wore her Lion King socks, which she thought made her stick out from the crowd. Luckily she had made friends with a very nice girl before school started who showed her the ropes and introduced her to everyone. She was a Danish girl who had experienced moving home as well.

It was surprising to see how many different nationalities of children went to this small African school. People come to Maun on contracts, or because their expertise is needed, and there is plenty of work for them here. Therefore as well as Batswana kids, there were children from South Africa, Zambia, China, Denmark, India, Zimbabwe, Sweden, the Faroe Isles, Germany, Australia and Britain. We quickly learned that the style of teaching was different to any we had known before. It was very 1950s British, blackboard teaching, with very little project work. We even had to learn a new style of writing and decimal points were written as commas. Geography was called Social Studies, and I remember feeling very foolish in one of these classes when I asked the teacher if Gaborone was a country, not knowing it was the capital of Botswana. My first class of Setswana, the national language, was even more embarrassing as I was given a textbook written for a five year old because I was so far behind. It had a picture of kittens on the front and I turned it face down on my desk so no one would notice it.

After classes we sat on the steps and ate our snack (there was no lunch hall or school food). We didn't talk much to anyone on that first day but we soon realised that the kids weren't that different after all and made friends quite quickly.

However, there was a bit of a problem with religion. During a discussion in class, every one was asked what their religion was. There were a whole range of religions including Hindu, Muslim and Christian. When it was Travers's turn, he said he was an atheist. This came as a terrible shock to them and a few days later when Travers walked into his classroom he found everyone praying for him and asking God not to let him burn in hell. As you can imagine, he was very surprised. He did not understand what the problem was, the teacher had readily accepted a variety of different faiths, so why did she find atheism so terrifying? He even found one of his friends in the playground crying for his soul. Trav was very distressed and confused by this and came home from school sobbing. The next day Mum attempted to reason with his teacher but to no avail. She found it hard to comprehend that such a sensible and nice woman was bringing up her children as atheists. It seemed to her that without religion there was no order and how would we know how to behave. To her, kindness and compassion stemmed from her faith, to us they are simply human qualities. Mum has taught us comparative religion and we know what a powerful role religions have played in world history. We also understand religion can offer comfort but we see no reason why atheism is so scary; it's just another way of looking at things.

In spite of some difficulties we stayed at Matshwane for two terms, as Mum wanted to give us a good chance to make friends and settle in. But Maisie and I continued to have problems with the different style of teaching. Maisie was dropped down a class. Her confidence plummeted and she became very unhappy. Travers was also struggling, because his dyslexia was not understood and as a result not acknowledged. Eventually there were so many problems that Mum decided to take us out of Matshwane and teach us herself. In all fairness, five years later Matshwane is an excellent school, thanks to the dedication of many committed teachers and parents.

The day we were taken out of school we had one of our big family meetings to discuss what should happen next. We have had family meetings all our lives. We gather around the table, Mum usually clutching a large mug of coffee, and each person gives their view on the subject of discussion. Sometimes we have huge disagreements and the whole thing degenerates (shouting, plates flying everywhere, you get the picture), but usually they are productive. When Mum first introduced the prospect of home school we weren't so sure it would work. While we were relieved to leave Matshwane we didn't want to leave our friends. However, at that time we lived next to the roller-blading rink (which, as Trav has mentioned, is the social hotspot for kids in Maun), and we felt confident our social life would not be affected. Another concern was whether Mum could do it. We knew she was a very intelligent person but she had no experience of primary school teaching (we were eight, eleven and twelve at the time) and she herself had doubts. She knew she would have only one chance to give us a good education, and she had to be confident that she could do it. After much discussion we decided to have a two-month trial period and then reassess. Such a radical change in our education would not have been so simple in England. But it was quite easy to get started, as there was no one from the

A geology lesson at the Matapos Hills, in Zimbabwe.

Social Services checking up on us and telling us what to do. All we had to do was to get the equipment, which was mainly stationery as we could not afford a computer, set up a working space at home and start.

I liked the idea of doing school in my own home for it would give us freedom; our school times are guided by the climate. In the summer we start in the cool of the morning at 6.30 a.m. and by 11.30 when it gets too hot to concentrate we stop. In the winter the mornings are very cold, and even starting as late as 8.30, we have to huddle under blankets for the first hour of school. However, as the morning progresses, layers of clothing are peeled off and at 1.30 when we finish we are down to shorts and t-shirts.

When the first day of home school arrived we were all excited and curious. Our first lesson ever was on geology, because Mum said that if we were going to learn about the world, we might as well understand how it was formed. We found she was excellent at making seemingly dull things interesting. I remember her pushing and pulling pieces of toffee around trying to explain plate tectonics and how mountains are formed (we were later allowed to eat our project).

Instead of looking at boring diagrams of moving particles, we actually got up and became atoms, huddling together as a solid and then running around the room more and more chaotically as we changed state from liquid to gas.

Mum proved to be an inspirational teacher and I think our understanding of the world has become much richer since she started to teach us. She has always explained to us the value of what we are learning and how we can put it to use. Since we have moved to the bush, our maths skills have become very useful. We can help to analyse the data from the lion survey and from the research. Learning how to take bearings is a crucial skill in the bush and brings trigonometry to life. She can even help us to see maths in nature. One morning we were asked to find examples of helices, spirals, Fibonacci numbers, fractals, symmetry, corresponding and alternate angles, and a myriad of other mathematical shapes all around camp. Our eyes were opened as we looked at the familiar plants, trees, insects, birds and holes in the sand searching for the hidden shapes. We found helices in kudu horns, an involute curve in an eagle's beak, alternate and corresponding angles in a leadwood branch and a tessellation in a mud wasp's nest.

While Mum teaches us all the conventional subjects, English, History, Geography, Biology, Maths, etc., she teaches them in an unusual way and integrates all subjects. We have learned that our past forms an integral part of our present. We are not just taught about the structure of a virus or bacteria but also how pathogens (organisms that causes disease) have shaped the path of history. I was interested to learn from *Plague's Progress* by Arno Karlen that in post-Plague Europe the Portuguese accidentally wiped out an entire race.

It all started when sugar, an Asian import, had been discovered as a sweetener. Sugar plantations were very labour intensive and European manpower had been wiped out by the Plague. The Portuguese searched for slave labour and discovered an isolated population of people known as the Guanches on the Canary Islands. The Guanches had been living in complete isolation for thousands of years and while they fought fiercely against the Portuguese they only had primitive Stone Age weapons and were soon defeated. However, in spite of their victory, the Portuguese went home without the slave labour they desired. They had killed some Gaunches in battle, but they killed far more, accidentally, by infecting them with everyday European germs like colds and flu. These diseases were lethal to the Guanches, as their immune systems had never come across them before. They died off rapidly and by 1600 there were only a few Hispano-Guanches left and now the race is extinct.

Pathogens even influence evolution, and by reading chapters from *The Red Queen* by Matt Ridley, we have come to understand the power of the parasite. Wherever possible Mum uses the lions as examples; their immune systems would not be as powerful as they are if they had not been continually challenged by a wide variety of parasites. Lions need to adapt constantly to stay ahead in the never-ending race between host and pathogen. Even Oakley is interested in parasites, which is not surprising, as he is always totally filthy. At one point he was infected with many tiny worms that lived just under his skin. He lovingly described them as his 'pets' as he squeezed them out. They eventually disappeared; he probably has one of the best immune systems of anyone in camp. One day, after Kate had collected a huge tapeworm from the poop of a female in the Santawani pride, he was fascinated to see how it worked and wanted to keep it in formalin.

All of this enriching does not come out of thin air. Mum often stays up till three in the morning figuring out how to make our lessons more inspiring. One of the things that have helped her most is our outstanding library. Luckily for us, she had prepared well and had brought a miscellany of books from England; people that come to camp are astounded by the diversity of the books on our shelves. She bought everything from *Mrs Tiggy-Winkle* to the *Cambridge Encyclopaedia of Human Evolution*. She wanted Oakley to have the same experiences we had as toddlers, so she brought *The Lion, the Witch and the Wardrobe*, *Winnie the Pooh* and all our other well-worn bedtime stories along. She wanted to bring books to satisfy our every mood or need, and had to think years ahead because she knew we would be growing up in Africa. Mum had an amazing literary background and she wanted us to share her love of the written word.

Before she became a biologist, Mum had been a Shakespearean actress and as a result can bring to life some very obscure poetry. Many children think of Shakespearean language as vastly complicated and tedious, but we have learned that Shakespeare is a terrific storyteller who can have us on the edge of our seats. It is hysterical to see Mum dancing around the tent, rushing in and out being different characters; she's great at accents so we don't get confused when she switches roles. Sometimes she gets so carried away it's hard to follow the plot and we have to go over the scene again. Oakley loves all the rushing about, sword fighting and decapitations.

Elephants on the Gomoti flood plain.

Shakespeare, Yeats, Louisa M. Alcott, Emily Dickinson, Arthur Miller, William Wharton and Lisa Carey are all in our library and have taught us history. At the moment we are reading *The Wild Swans* by Jung Chang and learning not only about the rise of communist China, but also about greed, lust for power, and the bonds between families and how the loss of culture affects the psychology and sanity of a nation. We are learning how quickly order breaks down without laws. Mao Zedong encouraged violence and killing, and let teenagers run wild with the closing down of schools, but it is incredibly moving to see how love and courage held a family together when everything around them was falling apart. This very personal biography gives us an insight into China's history in a way no textbook can because we can feel the people's pain, despair and hope. Even Oakley gets caught up in the story and his favourite person is the grandmother.

As Oakley got older he started to be taught alongside us. While we were being taught about photosynthesis and how plants turn sun light into sugar, he was just as fascinated and for proof he sucked on the end of wild flowers to see for himself how sweet the nectar was. Mum reads to him a lot; they have just finished *Jane Eyre*, and I remember the day he came out of the tent red-eyed after sobbing his heart out when Jane's school friend died. He was also very proud because it is a book none of us have read.

Over the years we have learned that home school is largely about self-motivation and enthusiasm. We have not been the only ones inspired by Mum's school. While we were living on the crocodile farm two boys named Shaks and Posta from Maun secondary school heard about our school and asked if they could join. Their Cambridge exams (equivalent to O-levels) were coming up and they wanted to get as much studying in as possible. They gave up their holidays to join our school and cycled twelve kilometres each way to join our classes. Mum helped them with their science and I remember Shaks wrote his first poem in our school. He was an excellent artist and in break time would produce wonderful drawings. It was great fun working together and we were very sad when they went back to secondary school.

The greatest example of enthusiasm and commitment to our school is given by Cathy Zerbe. This wonderful woman came into our life a year ago when Travers needed to start studying SAT maths to get into college in America. Mum saw that she herself was not capable of teaching maths at that level, and asked around town for a teacher that might coach him. Cathy offered to come to camp for a month as she loves the bush deeply, and in exchange she would give lessons. We all hit it off immediately, and within days she felt like family. We realised how special she was and she realised that we cared about what she was teaching. She and Mum became great friends and an arrangement was made that stretched both Mum's and Cathy's resources to the limit, but their passion to teach us was more important than anything. Cathy would come out to teach us for two days a week. This is an enormous feat. It takes one and a half hours along bumpy African roads to get to us and there may be elephant charges along the way. She drives alone at night in her ancient tin can of a car, with no one there for her if she has a puncture or a breakdown. After a while we managed to get her a car-to-car radio. Her car has little to no suspension and the risk of compressed vertebrae or severe brain damage while driving is high. When we hear her car coming towards camp we all spring to our feet. Oakley screams 'Cathy's here, Cathy's here!' and rushes outside to hug her. Her backseat is always stuffed full of fresh groceries and mail that she has managed to collect for us before setting out.

One of Cathy's greatest qualities is patience. When going over the same piece of maths for the seventh time, she shows no sign of frustration and keeps going till it has sunk in. Cathy has also livened up chemistry and biology with the many practicals and experiments she does with us. Before leaving for our camp, Cathy

loads up her cooler box with various bovine body parts, from lungs, livers and kidneys, to eyes and hearts; all these are later dissected in the back of her truck, diagrammed or used in organic chemistry experiments. Cathy is not just a teacher to us but a dear friend to Mum. They spend many happy hours together pooping the lions, getting lost in the dark and talking far into the night. We will always be grateful for all that she has done for us.

School doesn't just happen in the classroom. One of my best birthdays would not have been as full of wonder if I had not known something about geology and human evolution…

On the morning of my fourteenth birthday, over breakfast, I was handed the first clue to a treasure hunt. Birthday and Easter treasure hunts are a regular feature of our lives; Mum writes marvellously cryptic clues and hunts can last for hours. On this occasion each answer led me to a new destination along the route we were to take. The first letter of each answer had to be unravelled to reveal the name of the next place I was going to. As we headed south out of Maun I was totally discombobulated and we travelled for miles before I finally unmuddled the letters and found the answer, 'We're going to Jack's Camp!' I shouted.

Jack's Camp is in the middle of the Makgadikgadi Salt Pans. The pans lie at the north-eastern tip of the central Kalahari Desert and are the antithesis of the Okavango Delta. They are dry and barren, yet they have an ancient story to tell. Jack's is a beautiful camp, unlike any in Botswana. In one way it is very basic –

bucket showers and simple meru tents – yet it is also extremely comfortable. It has found the balance between simplicity and luxury but more importantly it feels like a home. In fact it originally was just that. A man named Jack Bousfield built the camp many years ago. He fell in love with the pans and would go out for days on end with a bit of food and drink on the back of his quad bike. His son Ralph grew up with the same passion for the pans, and when he took over the camp he decided to share it with other people and turn it into a tourist camp. After he married Katherine she took over the marketing side of the camp and made it well known. She, too, loved Jack's but suggested to Ralph that clients might want to have a little comfort, so she upgraded it a bit while still keeping it uncomplicated. They also employed wonderful people to work there and we received a warm welcome as we arrived.

We had an excellent lunch under the shade of a camelthorn tree, and were told that we would go out on to the salt pans later in the afternoon as the midday heat was overpowering. October is the hottest part of the year, and as the pans have no shade, the heat is reflected off the white sand, and it is easy to get seriously dehydrated. We pottered over to our tents to rest though I find it impossible to sleep in the afternoon – it's too boring. Finally, tea was served in a tent decorated in an Arabian style; there were big colourful carpets on the floor and we sat barefoot on the pillows that were scattered everywhere. After drinks and biscuits, Chris, our guide, told us to jump into the car and we set off towards the pans. After several kilometres we came upon a row of five quad bikes. I was really excited and couldn't wait to get on one of them. The only problem was I had never ridden one before and thought that it was going to be very difficult. However, Chris gave us very clear instructions and I felt reasonably confident. We were warned *never* to drive off the road because the ground was fragile and any tracks leading off the path would stay there until the next rainy season. Unlike quite a few of the camps in the Delta you feel that Jack's puts the environment first. Old Jack's love and respect for the pans is still there and kept alive.

People had tried to explain the Makgadikgadi pans to me before, but words are not enough. All they can say is that you see 'nothing'. 'Yeah, big deal?' you think. But as we drove over a rise and I saw them for the first time, it took my breath away. I'm going to try and explain what it's like but I'll probably not do any better than the rest. The salt pans are basically dried lake-beds from a once gigantic expanse of water (I will explain more about this later). When the water dried up it left behind tons of salts and minerals, making the ground uninhabitable for any plant life. The sand is a creamy colour and in the dry season every bit of moisture is sucked out of it, leaving it looking like a cracked piece of leather. The surface of the pans is covered in hexagonal shaped plates of minerals mixed with

sand. The salty crust glints in the sun, and as you put your foot down and break the thin, dry crust it sends up a fine white dust. For as far as you can see there is nothing, the horizon is not broken by anything and I swear you can see the curvature of the earth. We kept on driving, and because the road is so straight we picked up quite a pace without having to worry about crashing. Soon the sun started to set; now that was really something, watching an African sunset undisturbed by trees or houses while driving a bike across the pans.

Soon it became dark, and the air suddenly got icy cold. We slowed the pace down, switched on our headlights, and to our surprise we saw some lanterns in the distance. As the pans are totally uninhabited we couldn't figure out what it could be. As we got closer we found tables and chairs set out on the sand, and a small fire burning. The people in camp had set up a surprise birthday table in the middle of nowhere for us. I was astonished; I hadn't expected anything like that. Mum as usual burst into tears; it is hard to tell with my mother whether she is happy or sad as she cries at the drop of a hat. A while later, when we were huddled around the fire with a drink in our hands, Chris pulled out an old map and said, 'Now I'm going to tell you a bit about the pans.'

Imagine having a lecture about the evolution of the pans in a stuffy room illustrated by slides – I would have been asleep in seconds. But actually sitting on them, looking out into the wide open space and imagining the water glimmering under the moon was awe inspiring, I was fascinated. Tens of thousands of years ago (nobody knows the exact dates), Botswana was made up of huge lakes. The Okavango Delta, Lake Ngami and the Makgadikgadi Pans were all massive areas of water fed by huge rivers. Tectonic shifts diverted the rivers, and together with major climatic changes caused the lakes to shrink or dry up. The Delta is now a swamp, Lake Makgadikgadi is extinct and Lake Ngami is a shadow of its former self.

Birthday and Easter treasure hunts are a regular feature of our lives; Mum writes marvellously cryptic clues and hunts can last for hours. On this occasion each answer led me to a new destination along the route we were to take.

We had already learned at school that our hominid ancestors had probably followed rivers and lakes in search of food and water, but strangely scientists thought
that Stone Age hunter-gatherers had never inhabited Botswana. However, recent
discoveries of archaeological remains on extinct lake- and river-beds attracted
many archaeologists, and they soon found many Stone Age tools on the salt pans.
The tools were exposed and therefore easy to find because any dust that settled
on them was blown away. Early, middle and late Stone Age hominids made them.
The early Stone Age started about a million years ago and the late Stone Age
ended about 2000 years ago, when iron was discovered.

If you walk across the pans you are likely to come across a number of tools in
the shape of arrowheads. These tools were probably not used for arrows but to

cut the flesh of scavenged or hunted prey. Even now, after thousands of years you can still feel the sharpness of their edges. These tools have raised many mysteries. There are quite a few theories as to how they got there, I think the most probable is that they were carried by ancient rivers. The discovery of enormous 'axe heads' (these too are shaped like arrowheads but can be a metre long) had people guessing. Some people thought they were lugged into trees by hominids and dropped on to animals' heads, but it seems more likely they used them in some kind of ritual. It is astonishing to touch a tool that a Stone Age man has held in his hand. It is even more remarkable to imagine that the mitochondrial DNA floating around in my body could have been passed on to me through that same tool maker's maternal line.

Chris looked up at the darkened sky and asked us if we wanted to run. We all looked at him as if he was mad. Having lived so long in the bush it was instilled into us that no one should walk about at night. He told us to run out as far as we could and then lie down and look at the stars. We looked at Mum but she was already up and ready to go. So we started sprinting out into the dark. All we could see were the stars and all we could feel was the ground pounding under our feet

and the wind on our faces. We ran flat out for ages, completely free, until we could barely see the fire behind us. It was the most incredible feeling being able to run through the night without a care in our minds. Finally, exhausted, lying stretched out looking up at the sky, I felt I was floating in space. It was the constant giggles and shuffles of Oakley moving from person to person that brought us back to reality. Soon we jogged back to the fire expecting to have to pack up the tables and chairs, but Chris told us it would be taken care of, so we were able to keep the feeling in our stomachs that you get after you've had an amazing experience.

The following morning I was asked whether I wanted to go on a game drive or back to the Pans. We laughed at the idea of a game drive, we get enough of that at home. So after being loaded up with cool drinks and snacks we were soon back on the quad bikes. The cool breeze on our faces was very refreshing and any sleepiness was blown away. We soon discovered that tools were not the only things to be found on the pans. Maisie found something called a root cast: these are white, tubular, solid structures made out of calcium. They are formed after a tree dies and its root starts to rot. Calcium is filtered through the ground into the space made by the root and eventually becomes so compact it forms a cast, almost like plaster of Paris over a broken arm.

Chris then showed us an old marking left by a brown hyena. The spotted hyenas we see in the Delta are in a different genus, and brown hyenas are more solitary, though they do have social dens. They paste grass stalks with a brown secretion from their anal glands to mark their territory, over time this turns white. We also found an amazing desert-adapted beetle. Its wing case was fused together so there was no way it could fly. As insects lose water through the opening in their wing cases, the function of this adaptation is to enable the beetle to retain as much moisture as possible in a very arid environment. So far Jack's has been my best birthday. I learned so much, and now have memories that will be with me forever. The car journey back was virtually silent as we all went over the incredible experience in our minds. Jack's will always be with us.

Many people wonder if we are getting enough culture by living in the bush. I think the culture we get here is so little understood that it remains a mystery to most people. I would rather have a birthday at Jack's Camp than at Alton Towers any day. I'm not saying the education we get here is better than everyone else's, it's just different. There are things I miss, like sport, languages (Mum is a hopeless linguist), friends to work with, well-equipped laboratories and music. I would like to learn how to play more musical instruments. But we see things you can never find in a classroom, we see the point of what we are learning, and we have far more freedom to explore. Even though it's not perfect, I'd rather have this amazing school and wonderful teacher than any other in the world.

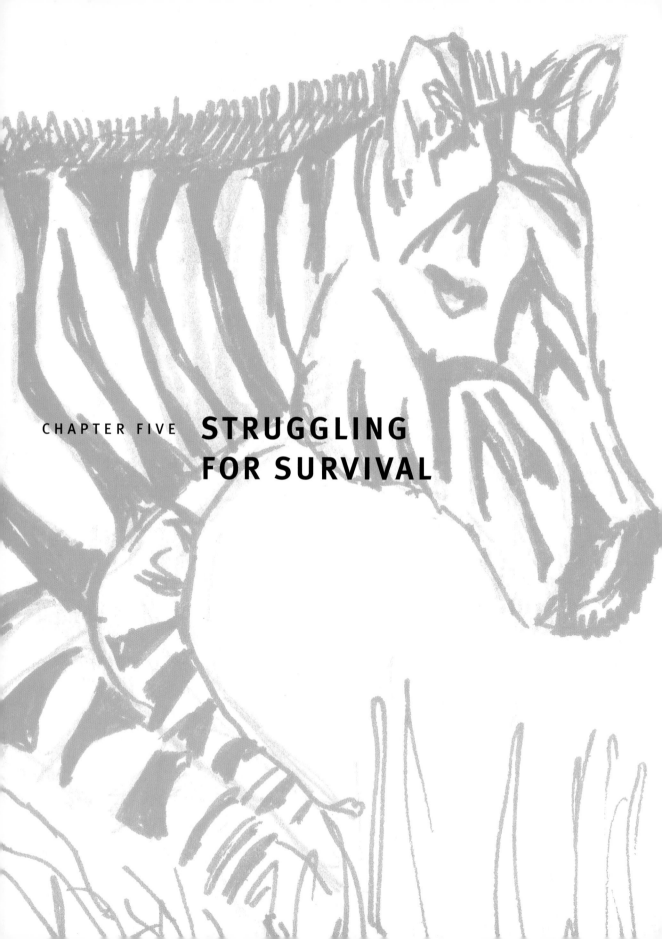

CHAPTER FIVE **STRUGGLING FOR SURVIVAL**

CHANGING PERSPECTIVES

ANGUS

WHEN I USED TO LOOK UP at the night sky and saw all the millions of stars I felt hugely insignificant. Just to think – our galaxy is made up of more than ten billion stars (our sun being a relatively small one). Many of these stars have solar systems, just like ours. This is all inside one galaxy, there are myriads more. Then, on top of that, place the idea of even more universes. And we are still hugely in the dark about our own solar system; even our nearest planet has not been explored. When I thought of all this, my mind burst.

However, recently I read a piece by Martin Rees in a book called *How Things Are*, and I learned something that changed my perspective. He explains: all the atoms flung into space by supernovae, after wandering through the cosmos for hundreds of millions of years, might form a dense interstellar cloud which collapses under its own gravity to make new stars, some with solar systems. So, therefore, the atoms in your body have once been inside a star.

'We are star-dust – the ashes of long dead stars,' that sentence changed my thinking. Now when I look up at the stars they feel less out of reach, more a part of me.

Four years ago, when I was ten and a half, standing in the middle of the Delta, at night and lost, I felt the same kind of stellar insignificance. As the lions roared in the distance I suddenly felt like an intruder. Life didn't pivot around human beings any more, as it had once seemed; this was their world, a world in which I didn't belong. Suddenly, all my senses were awake. The boy whose walks in England had consisted of piggybacks, climbing trees and falling in cowpats was now nervously alert. Every

sound was magnified tenfold – the snap of a twig had me looking around attentively. I started to hear things that I had ignored on previous walks: the plop of a cat fish as it surfaced to catch a water boatman, the tinkling of the bell frogs, the chirping of crickets and the deep 'hoom, hoom' of the giant eagle owl. I noticed bush babies jumping through the trees, peering down on me with their big, spooky eyes. And then the eerie 'whoop' of the hyenas, the high-pitched, mournful wail of the jackal, followed by the deep, booming roar of the lion froze my blood. As I walked on the moonlit land, all I wished was that I had not left the car.

Trav and I had been travelling to a camp in the Delta on the back of a supply truck with some family friends. However, our truck had broken down five hours into our journey. One of the adults in the group said we weren't far from camp, which lay close to the river, and he knew the way. I felt a tinge of fear as I realised he meant us to walk. Walking went against my instincts and we had been taught always to stay with our vehicle in the bush. If I were put into that situation now I would sleep in the back of the truck and wait for help, but aged ten I was inexperienced and scared and wanted to stick with the adults.

After an hour of walking, the two men in the group announced they were lost. My stomach felt like it had been replaced by a pound of lead. The sun had just gone down, and it wasn't just the predators that I was worried about, the place was also teeming with elephant and buffalo. However, we kept on walking through the dusk in the direction he thought best. Soon the moon rose and the roars and whoops surrounded us. It was decided it would be too dangerous to carry on so we were going to camp out in the forest ahead of us. The plan was to lay some blankets down on the ground, light a fire and sleep in the open.

As we approached the forest we caught a glimpse of moonlight reflected in water. We had found the river and surely the camp was nearby. I felt hugely relieved and walked on with more of a bounce in my step. This was short lived. One of my friends stopped dead in his tracks; 'Elephant', he said in a low voice. A bull elephant was dead ahead of us blocking our path. We tried to move around the animal as inconspicuously as possible but seven people were hard to hide and just as we thought we had made it, the elephant came straight for us. We knew this was not a mock charge – the head was down and the ears were out, it wasn't going to stop. Terror struck us as the dark, massive bulk moved down on us. I was about to leap out of the way when one of the adults shouted, 'everyone stick together and scream your heads off'.

That advice probably saved my life. As we had no chance of outrunning the elephant, the idea was to scare him off; elephants hate big noises and by bunching together we looked like one large animal. We all yelled our hearts out and waved our blankets frantically. Luckily the elephant did not sense our fear, he lost his nerve and skidded to a halt five metres in front of us, then he turned on his heel and sped off into the forest. My knees fractured they were shaking so much. I had never been charged on foot by elephant before and it's not something I would like to experience again! Animals look as if they are twice their size at night and it took a while for our legs to return from their jelly-like state.

Moments later we saw lights twinkling on the other side of the river and we called across to the people in the camp. They sounded surprised to hear us and soon paddled a canoe over to collect us. Relief swamped me as I climbed into the little wooden canoe, called a Mokoro; it almost felt like coming home. We glided silently across the gently flowing water and on the other side we were given a hot meal and a soft mattress to sleep on. After all that it turned out to be the wrong camp anyway, the camp we had been aiming for was kilometres away. The last thing our rescuers had expected to see that night were three grown-ups and four bedraggled children appearing out of nowhere, and everyone gathered around the fire to hear our story.

I learned many things from this experience, not to leave your vehicle and walk at dusk being the most obvious. Much more importantly I gained a deep respect for the animals, and looked at them in a different light. I realised they are not just there for our entertainment, but are struggling to stay alive in a rough environment. On that adventure I learned how seriously walking in the bush should be

undertaken. A good walk, which is a safe walk, depends not just on the knowledge of the guide, but largely on the obedience of the guided.

Twenty years ago, most guides had grown up in the bush. Sadly this old breed of Botswana guides is slowly waning as more and more children are being taken out of the bush and sent to towns to get educated; as a result they are losing touch with their roots. While Western education is providing much that's needed it is also taking something away that can never be replaced: a childhood in the bush.

Children notice things that adults never do. I have been taught to use my senses by friends like Tim Longdon, David and Roger Dugmore, Sean Watson, Adrian Dandridge, Jeff Gush, Julian Cook, Kamunga, MD, Conrad and many others, all of whom have grown up in Africa. They have lived, smelled, touched and breathed it all their lives. As toddlers they crawled in sand and noticed all the insects, as children they climbed trees and watched the birds and as young men they hunted with their fathers and learned to read the animals. Their respect, knowledge and love for the bush are inspirational. They

Dung beetle.

can keep me interested for hours exploring a piece of land of not more than one hundred square metres. I have watched vicious fights between Matabele ants and bees, seen praying mantis stalking their prey and mud wasps bring back paralysed jumping spiders to their nests to feed their young. I have spent hours watching dung beetles patiently rolling huge dung balls, and have learned how to identify black-shouldered kites as they hover over a plain looking for mice – all the little things that you miss sitting in the back of a truck. Bush walking should be used to see these small pieces of nature.

It saddens me when people come to Africa simply to see the 'Big Five' (lion, buffalo, elephant, leopard and rhino). They are missing the whole world of small things. Strangely people are scared of them. They squash harmless wall spiders in their tents, not knowing that these spiders are just as effective at killing mosquitoes as the spray they have bought along. They look at side-striped sand snakes, one of the most beautiful creatures in Africa, with revulsion, wrongly thinking they're slimy and poisonous. But oddly some people think nothing of trying to get close to dangerous game on foot.

If you go on a walk looking for big game, you are also looking for trouble. Many camps in the Delta allow guides to carry rifles on walks to protect their clients. Armed walking is

Praying mantis.

OPPOSITE Bush walking with our friends Dougie and Sandie's trained elephants.

not as responsible as it seems. Tourists can feel a false sense of security because they have the safety of a weapon, so they urge their guide to take them closer to the animal for a better photograph, or they just want to stay that little bit too long with the creature. A step too close or a moment too long and the dangerous animal may feel threatened, charge out of fear and get shot. For what? So a client can get a good picture or have an adrenaline rush? I think this is a tragic waste of a beautiful animal's life. In the five years that I have been here I know of two elephants, four lions, a buffalo and two hippos that have been killed to defend clients on walking safaris. Much of this could have been prevented if the people had kept their distance. I wonder if they thought their walks were worth it.

Don't get me wrong, I think bush walking is fantastic, if it is done in the right way, unarmed and with a deeply experienced guide who is wise enough to keep out of danger. Once we were lucky enough to walk in the Delta with trained elephants and their guides. Some camps in the Delta do not allow cars, for they harm the fragile environment, and mokoro rides and bush walking provide an environmentally friendly alternative. It is intense being on the same level as the animals; you can hear the bush uncontaminated by the noise of a car and smell it without the scent of fuel.

I will never forget the Boxing Day walk we had in the Delta. It was our second African Christmas and Oakley was only three. Our guides were Kamunga, an old man with a weather-beaten face, and MD who was much younger with a different kind of wisdom and authority about him. They worked in sync, trusting each other's skills, and they were not dependent on a weapon. They walked with long strides, slowly, silently, their bare feet feeling the ground beneath them. Kamunga steered us clear of long grass and forest and spotted antelopes in the distance that none of us had seen. All the while MD was looking out for tracks and dung on the ground and listening intently to the faintest sounds. Oakley could see further than any of us since he was perched happily on Kamunga's shoulders, with his hands holding tightly to his wiry grey hair.

After a while they came upon lion tracks and stopped. Kamunga asked us if we wanted to follow them. If I was asked now, I would say no. I now know how lions' moods change from day to day and how unpredictable they can be. But back in our early days the offer was too exciting to turn down and we trusted that Kamunga would not take any risks with us. MD took the lead, following the spoors expertly; he could see the slightest print in the sand beneath thick grass. Kamunga walked with us, watching our every move. I think he was seeing if we would be able to hold our nerve around the lions. We followed MD for about two hundred metres until we reached the forest line. Our guides were looking around them acutely aware and led us to stand behind a big termite mound.

Kamunga asked us to poke our heads carefully around the mound and there, forty metres in front of us were ten lions inside a thick bush. Some of them were chewing on the remains of a warthog. They had all seen us and stared straight ahead at the termite mound, as if their sight penetrated it. We held our breath and Kamunga slid Oakley from his shoulders into his arms and held him close. Oakley felt no fear leaning against the old man's chest, feeling his steady breathing. Something spooked the lions and they all got up. We froze but breathed a sigh of relief as they jogged away from us across the plain. Kamunga however remained tense and told us to look deeper into the grass. A female with two cubs by her side was staring at us intently, her tail flicking in the air. Her ears were laid back on her head and her body was flat to the ground, ready to pounce. She was telling us that if we moved one step closer to those cubs, she would charge. Wordlessly Kamunga guided us slowly away; his authority mesmerised the group and we moved as one. We made our way safely back on to the plain and Oakley was once again returned to Kamunga's shoulders showing us that all was well.

We all placed our trust in good hands. However, there are animals that even the best guides cannot read; a year later Kamunga was taken by a crocodile. His wisdom, heart and skill are sorely missed in the Delta.

Life is full of risks. A paddler in a mokoro in the Delta is taking just as many risks as a Gloucestershire farmer working with animals and heavy machinery. However there is a big difference. Medical help is close at hand for the farmer; all he has to do is to reach a telephone. On the other hand the paddler is stranded in the swamps, in a dangerous environment, hours away from the nearest hospital, with no means of communication. This is the situation we live in. It was Allison Brown, who Travers has talked about, that told Mum to get her act into gear. She said that it was irresponsible to have lived in the bush for so long and not to have done a medical course. She invited her to come to town immediately and do the intensive four-day course she had devised. Mum knew Allison was right and felt ashamed. To tell the truth, the reason she hadn't done the course was because she knew she would have to practise an intravenous injection on a person.

I really wanted to do the course and Allison agreed it was important to have two people in camp that were trained. It was an eye-opening experience. The course covered all the standard first-aid things: CPR (cardio-pulmonary resuscitation), how to deal with fractures, burns, haemorrhages, head injuries, emergency child birth, the ABCs of trauma etc., but it was very much 'bush' orientated, being designed to help us to stabilise someone who may have been wounded under horrific conditions, for many hours without help. What drove me through the hard bits of the course was that I knew the skills I was learning could save my family.

Dehydration can be as serious as blood loss in a hot climate, and Allison taught us how to set up a rehydrating intravenous drip. In England this would be illegal for an unqualified person to do, but out here it is a life-saving skill. After days of putting a needle into a plastic arm, Mum and I had to practise on each other. I was terrified that I would hurt her but knew I had to keep calm, for a shaking hand was the last thing she needed. Mum placed her trust in me, which was very brave, and I did it in one. Mum found it harder to do that to her own son, however, and went through my vein, at which point she burst into tears and a fellow trainee kindly volunteered his arm. She did it first time.

If I had done a first-aid course in England I might not have taken it so seriously, because I would have been confident that in a dire emergency professional help would have been nearby. But who was there to help us out in the middle of the Okavango? Given our work with lions, dealing with large animal bites was something we might well have to face. Mum and I listened intently to Allison's instructions, hoping all the while we would never have to put them into practice. She also covered protocols for snakebites and scorpion stings, a reality in Africa, though not as common as people think. A scorpion has stung me and it was one of the most painful things I have ever endured.

The scorpion that stung Angus.

I had been playing table tennis in bare feet and at first I thought I had trodden on a thorn, a regular occurrence in our bare-foot life. However, a few seconds later, it felt as though hundreds of red-hot needles were travelling through my veins as the venom seeped into my foot. Looking down, I saw a large black scorpion, four and a half inches long, with small pincers and a large tail, with its sting embedded in my toe. I was scared because I knew this species injects the most potent venom. While I was writhing on the ground holding my foot and screaming, Travers killed the creature and rushed to radio Mum and Pieter who sped back from the lions. Meanwhile, Trav submerged my foot in iced water to reduce the swelling, and gave me Rescue Remedy for shock. The pain got worse with time, as the venom oozed through my body, spreading in agonising pins and needles right up to my neck. On arrival Mum gave me a strong antihistamine, as my throat had by then started to swell up. Without these pills it could have got quite serious.

Pieter took a look at the scorpion. We have been taught to keep specimens wherever possible for identification, as not all species are dangerously toxic. To maintain calm he reassured me it could do no harm; but later he told me he had been very worried, as these scorpions had been known to kill babies. The venom

Corrie has battled like an old lion, living on breakfast and beer, throwing off malaria and other ailments with confidence. We would like to thank him for donating his magnificent wildlife and bush photographs.

is neuro-toxic and can affect the respiratory system. The swelling around the bite site may also cause nerve damage. Mum, Pieter and Travers knew the most important medicine in any emergency is not to panic; many of the fatalities due to bites or stings are caused by fear-induced shock. I was told to take it easy for the next few hours but by the evening I was well recovered, though the pins and needles stayed for several days. At no time during this episode did Mum or Pieter feel the need to call Allison, they knew they could handle the situation, they didn't want to worry me and there might have been someone else on her line who needed life-saving advice. While Pieter had malaria, the class Allison was running at the time was interrupted many times by our radio calls.

The medical course gave me confidence. It was nice to know that at fourteen I was keeping up in a class of many people older than me. At the end of it Mum and I were changed people. We had been asked to explore some huge moral dilemmas. In a situation involving more than one patient we had been taught to assess which patient needed the most attention and, worse, which patient was beyond our help – impossible how to choose a stranger over a family member. How do you help a stranger and know that a family member is nearby, dying? This was a question that we had to face. In a situation like that, emotions that are almost impossible to overcome have to be put aside, and the right thing has to be done; choose the person who has a chance, choose the person that you can do something for in the middle of nowhere.

Mum and I have had to use the skills we learned, though luckily, not under such horrifying conditions.

One evening in the rainy season, we were having supper when we heard a car shunting down the driveway. Anne, the manager of Gomoti Camp, rushed in looking pale and shaken up. 'What is it?' we asked anxiously.

'Please help,' she said in a high-pitched voice, 'Corrie has smashed his knee.'

We found Corrie propped awkwardly up against the wall of his meru tent, his legs splayed out across the concrete floor. He looked pale and sweaty, 'Hello,' he whispered in a weak voice, 'I slipped, and I think the plate in my knee has been dislodged.'

Corrie is an elderly man, and his right leg was badly damaged in a car crash many years ago. He had to have a plate put in his knee and a brace to correct his twisted leg. In spite of this he goes on living a tough bush life, because he loves the animals with all his heart. He told us that the pain spread from his hip to his toes. Mum and I did not notice any disfigurement, indicating a break, but it was hard to be sure for the limb was fragile and had still not fully recovered from the crash.

First things first, I got on to the radio, while Travers got blankets and pillows. Corrie needed to be made warm and comfy, as he was still lying on a cold concrete floor that was about to flood from the heavy rain beating down outside. Mum stayed to comfort and examine him; meanwhile Anne made him some tea, a break from his customary beer! I ran through the pelting rain to the Land Rover, and radioed Allison:

— Allison Brown, Allison Brown.
— Copy.
— Hi Allison, this is Angus McNeice at Gomoti Camp. Corrie has badly
    damaged his leg. We cannot see or feel any breaks and there is no swelling
    or blood under the skin. He says it feels like he has slipped the metal disc
    in his knee, over.
— Okay, Angus, you know the drill for a damaged leg, splint both legs together.
    Tell me what painkillers you have, keep the leg stable, get him comfy and
    keep me informed, tell me all that happens. I don't think we will be able
    to get the chopper out in this weather at night, it'll come first thing tomorrow
    morning. Will you be all right Angus? Over.
— Okay, copy Allison, we'll be fine, over.

I really had to concentrate on the radio, because Allison's strong Scottish accent is hard enough to understand face to face, let alone over a crackling radio. I relayed the message to Mum and rummaged through the medical box for the painkillers. I found some ibuprofen and Synap-Forty. Mum asked Anne if Corrie was allergic to anything or had any ailments. She said he had bad stomach ulcers, and that part of his stomach had previously been removed. I went back to the radio:

— Allison, Allison this is Angus.
— Go ahead, Angus.
— We have ibuprofen or Synap-Forty, but Corrie has bad stomach ulcers.
— Okay Angus, use the Synap-Forty, copy?
— Copy that Allison, we should use Synap-Forty.
— A-firm, Angus, you are doing well, over.

After we gave him the painkiller we set about immobilising the leg. We gathered bandages and two pillows, and then slowly bought his legs together, trying to keep movement to a minimum. Even so, he grimaced with pain and puffed frantically on his pipe. We placed the two pillows in between his legs and then started to tie the legs together. We wanted to use the unharmed leg as a splint so he could not bend or move the other. After ten agonising minutes we managed to splint him.

As I said earlier, there was no sign of a break, swelling or any irregularities in his pulse from the femoral artery that would indicate torn arteries. Therefore, with Allison's agreement, we decided a drip was not needed. Corrie was thanking us all the time, and apologising for interrupting our evening! By now the rain was coming down in buckets and he was lying near a rapidly forming puddle. He could not spend the night like that, and though he begged not to be moved, we knew we had to get him on to his bed. Pieter improvised a stretcher using a folding metal table and laid it down next to him. Corrie was very scared that we were going to hurt him, but we carefully rolled his body on to the table while he gritted his teeth. Finally we got him as comfortable as possible under the circumstances. We snuggled him under a blanket and for the first time that night he looked peaceful.

I called Allison once again and she said Corrie would be fine for the night but that we should check on him regularly. After kissing Anne goodbye and reassuring her, we went home and had a good night's sleep, apart from Mum who went over every five seconds to check up on him.

The next morning the helicopter arrived. As it landed outside Gomoti Camp the whole community gathered to watch. Oakley was ecstatic and had to be held back from running towards the propeller blades. We were nervous while the paramedic examined Corrie, we hoped we hadn't done anything wrong. We were greatly relieved to hear that he would be fine and that we had done a good job. We watched the chopper carrying Corrie fly into the distance, safe in the knowledge that he would be taken care of. He was sent to Gaborone where an X-ray revealed that he had split his femur from hip to knee. He must have endured incredible pain that night, yet the brave man never complained.

He is back in camp now but still recovering and itching to find the lions that he loves so much. Although Corrie has fine bird bones he is made of very tough stuff, or he couldn't have survived living so long in the bush. He has battled like an old lion, living on breakfast and beer, throwing off malaria and other African ailments with confidence. And like any successful male lion, he has been able to find a partner late in life. He and Anne fell in love four years ago. She is a remarkable woman who shares his love for the bush and has shown great courage in leaving her comfortable Johannesburg life and choosing to live in a leaky meru tent on the edge of the Gomoti river without complaint.

Unlike Corrie, most people that visit our camp suffer from a syndrome we call Pathogen Paranoia. They arrive from the First World pumped full of unnecessary vaccines and prophylactics, clutching their water purification tablets and having ignored our accurate and yet minimalist directions on health care. Instead they prefer to listen to the dire warnings issued by well-meaning health officials, who insist that Africa is a cesspit of millions of life-threatening diseases and that they can't be too careful. It is wonderful to see their anxieties melt away over time and soon they learn to trust good clean dirt. However, there is one disease that is rarely discussed by our visitors and yet poses the greatest threat of any pathogen: HIV.

Botswana has the highest rate of HIV transmission of any country in the world. One in three of its people are infected. That statistic is quite shocking, isn't it? That means that one third of the people that I meet, play with, laugh with, work with and talk with could have a virus that will kill them, and could kill me if I am careless. In many developed countries HIV-positive kids are often ostracised in the playground, but how can you ostracise a third of 1.5 million people? The answer is you don't. You try to help them in any way possible.

AIDS has shocked the nation. The Batswana do not show emotion very easily and it is rare to see someone crying. However, we have seen some of our good friends collapse with grief as they receive the news that yet another of their relatives has died. Bring, who helps us in camp, lost four of his close family in one year to the 'Botswana Sickness' (AIDS-related tuberculosis and diarrhoea).

AIDS orphanages are opening all over the country as more and more children are left stranded, unable to be supported by rapidly dwindling families. Here in Maun the Lutheran Church has opened a day-care centre. Some of these children may themselves be infected with HIV and the centre aims to give all the children as good a time as possible and improve the quality of their life. Many people in town, who have no money for donations but want to make a difference, are trying to help by any means they can. A group of our friends from Maun are building a playground for the kids. And we have invited the children out to camp to see animals they have never seen before.

Travers, Maisie, Oakley and I have learned that we do not need to be afraid of AIDS. HIV is hard to catch – there is no risk in hugging, shaking hands, breathing the same air, sharing a glass and playing with a person who is HIV positive. You can only be infected through blood and other bodily fluids. However, we need to be sensible and aware that HIV is a reality in our lives. In camp we have to take responsibility for our own health care as well as other people's, as we often have to clean up cuts and grazes. Putting on a pair of latex gloves beforehand is second nature now.

When we lived in England we were taught about AIDS, but it didn't really affect us in any way. In Botswana it is happening right in front of us. We are watching people we have known for five years wasting away before our eyes. We have seen the number of funeral processions through town increase over the years.

A funeral is a profoundly important event in Botswana, and it is an insult not to have the entire family present, even distant relatives. Also a cow must be slaughtered both as a mark of respect and to feed the mourners. As the number of cattle a person owns measures their wealth, slaughtering four or five cows a year is a very serious matter. This has caused confusion because cultural practice now presents practical problems. Bring now has the additional responsibility of several grandchildren who have been orphaned by AIDS. How many more cows can he lose? A simple yet moving consequence of the AIDS crisis is that it is no longer considered an insult to slaughter a lowly goat at a funeral.

HIV is killing off the working population as well as the children, and shockingly over eighty per cent of the students at the University of Botswana are HIV positive. This means that future lawyers, politicians, scientists, teachers, wildlife officers, doctors, nurses and other key individuals involved in the further development of Botswana may be dead in the next ten years. What chance does the country have if its work force is diminished that badly? The Botswana government has to deal with a serious problem if its country is to have a future.

The last time I went back to England there was nothing on the news about how HIV is killing people in many African countries. If the more dramatic Ebola virus infected Botswana, the media would be right on top of it. But HIV kills slowly over time; the drama of HIV is private. Families in Botswana are used to living with another killer disease, malaria; they understand it, recognise the symptoms and can take action. However AIDS has no specific symptoms and many people don't associate the 'Botswana Sickness' with HIV; this leaves them vulnerable.

Another problem is that people earn so little that they cannot afford the expensive medication that could help them. Our wonderful Doctor Patrick is in despair as more and more cadaverous people come into his office in agony. They sit for half an hour as he offers them his friendship and patience, and restores their dignity. It must be distressing to be a doctor in a country where people are dying from a disease that as yet has no cure. Patrick is training as an acupuncturist and a homeopath, trying to find some affordable ways to help these frail people.

While acupuncture and homeopathy may alleviate symptoms and pain and give some hope, they cannot cure AIDS. It is going to be very interesting to meet a friend of Pieter's who is a geneticist and world leader in trying to find a cure for AIDS. Dr Steve O'Brian is coming to camp to discuss FIV infection in lions. Steve believes there might be something to learn from lions, who seem to combat FIV more successfully than humans combat HIV. What systems are at work within the lions? Answers to questions like this might help millions of people. Five years ago, in England, all this would have meant nothing to me. But now I live in a country were both HIV and FIV are rampant and I will be fascinated to hear what he has to say; as it is very exciting to think that work with wild animals might be able to help people as well.

So much has changed since I stepped off that plane five years ago, into a country that I knew nothing about. Now it has become a home that I love and care for. People often ask me which I prefer, England or Africa, but it is not possible to compare the two. It is like asking me which is better, pizza or chocolate mousse. They both taste good but they are made from completely different ingredients and, like the two foods, I want England and Botswana at different times. However, if someone forced me to choose between my two homes, which I hope never happens, I would choose Africa. I see myself with a future here. I don't know what lies ahead for me or how my thinking may change. But I do know the largest life-changing event in my life has been working with the lions and meeting Pieter.

It has opened new horizons for me and now I realise how different researching animals is simply to loving them. We are trying to understand lions. We observe everything they do, ask ourselves why they are doing it and what makes that possible. By doing this we are not taking the wonder away from them. By looking deeper into them, and striving to see how they work, they have become more wonderful in my eyes. And by attempting to enrich our understanding, we have a better chance of saving the lions. This is what I want to do when I grow up: I want to work with nature. It may not be in Botswana – it could be in South America or Asia – but it will be somewhere wild, where the animals are free.

THE FAMILY
MAISIE

SHE WALKED OFF THE PLANE leaning on her stick with one hand and waving with the other. She walked with a slight wobble but tried with all her might not to show it.

Our grandmother Facey has hit seventy and lives each day with joy and passion and doesn't waste a minute of it. Facey is actually named Faith, but when Emily was younger she couldn't pronounce 'Faith' and Facey stuck.

This was her first visit to Africa, and we were all so happy to see her. Since Pieter and my grandmother had never met, this visit was a great chance for them to get to know one another. We took her to lunch so she could rest after her long journey but she was impatient, as she was itching to see her first African animals. I wondered if, like Mum, she would burst into tears at the sight of her first impala. Once we were through the buffalo fence we started to see animals, giraffes, impalas, ostriches and an elephant – which she missed, as she was looking the other way. It seemed as if all the animals in Africa were parading for Facey and she was overjoyed.

Back in camp Facey was amazed that her tent had a proper bed, a table, a lamp and places to put her things; everything made her happy. Later that evening we sat down to a candle-lit dinner as we always do. Suddenly we heard lions calling in the distance, they were quite far away, and we made sure we told Facey that. But she wasn't afraid and she listened to them fascinated. It gives me such joy to see people so astonished by every little thing they see and hear in the bush. I was once like them, so interested in every impala. I hate to admit it but I have lost most of that now. Don't get me wrong: I love the animals and find lots of things interesting in the Delta, but I've got used to hearing lions roar, and each bird's call no longer fascinates me. Just walking through an English forest is as interesting to me as a lion is to a tourist out here.

After we had finished supper Facey asked Mum to take her to the long drop. As you know, we drive everywhere at night, as lions, leopards and hyenas regularly walk through camp. Facey's 'real African adventures' started that night. Mum shone the light of the car on the long drop in order to keep her safe, but once they were ready to go and she tried to start the car, the battery had gone flat. Travers and Pieter were on their way to 'rescue' them when they heard the famous clunck clunck of a flat tyre; great, and they were only half way across camp! They got out the high-lift jack and changed the tyre, while Mum and her mother were having a wonderful time chatting, reading magazines collected from

Male Impala. Even though we see them every day we still stop to stare at these intensely beautiful animals.

the long drop and giggling hysterically. All was solved and finally they could go and pick up my grandmother. They drove her, exhausted at last, to bed.

The next morning we wanted her to have a lie in and planned to give her a relaxing day. Well, to hell with that, she was up really early and asking when they were off to find lions. Mum and Pieter took her to find the Mogogelo pride. The Mogogelo is my favourite place, it is peaceful and all the animals are attracted to the breathtaking river. Facey was thrilled and took thousands of pictures with her 'sixteenth century' pocket camera, with which she had to be about fifteen inches away from the animals and even then they looked like dots.

My grandmother had only seen Africa on BBC documentaries narrated by David Attenborough; she couldn't believe her luck that she was actually seeing the real thing. She began to get very weepy in the presence of such beauty and silence but before she could let the wonder sink in they came upon a pride of lions. To enrich her excitement the pride was unknown to us. Facey was deeply moved by the lions. She is in no way a soppy woman but like most people she was overwhelmed to see a real wild lion in front of her for the first time.

When I saw my first lions I got an adrenaline rush and I couldn't take my eyes off them. I can't exactly remember how I felt; I know that sounds quite weird but I do spend nearly every day with them and my memories seem to blend. Once you actually know the lions you feel much closer to them. And it is possible they recognise us. The other day Mum and I went to check up on Krystal to see if she had had her cubs. I was driving and when we came upon her she looked at us in a strange way.

'She knows it's you,' said Mum. She explained Krystal wasn't used to seeing me in the driver's seat. I still don't know if that's true but it is nice to think that the lions know who each of us is.

By the time Mum and Pieter had identified each new lion it was dusk. You would think that Facey would be exhausted after a twelve-hour plane trip and on top of that being stuffed in the car for hours on end, but no way, not my grandmother. They finally headed home… or so they thought. The Mogogelo has overgrown roads that are hard to keep track of at night and Pieter drove around in circles for an hour, trying to avoid falling in the swamps. Finally he admitted that he was hopelessly lost. Faith's eyes widened, she clutched Mum's arm tightly and said,

'If a man admits he's lost, then he's a real man.'

Mum smiled while Pieter glowed with pride. Shortly afterwards Mum turned to her mother and said,

'I'm sorry darling, but there is a high possibility that we will spend the night out here;' at which point a hippo burst out of the bushes and charged them.

Hippos run extremely fast in spite of their short legs and can damage a car to distraction.

'Don't worry, darling; that will be fine,' replied my grandmother, but her smile was waning. Fortunately it was only a mock charge, and the hippo came to a standstill.

Much to their relief Pieter announced that he had recognised a tree line in the distance. After manoeuvring through a thick forest they hit a well-defined road and were soon safely at camp. Facey felt very proud of her first day in the bush.

The next morning she arrived in the kitchen dressed from ear to toe in yellow. Yellow top, yellow trousers, yellow shoes, yellow beads and yellow earrings. This gave me a lot of joy. She had woken up to the sound of Mum scaring away elephants by banging a wooded spoon against a colander. We don't want elephants to get habituated to camp, for our safety and theirs. In another camp we have seen a habituated elephant shot as a problem animal and it sickened us. Facey found this elephant shooing hugely amusing, and it wasn't long before she was doing it herself, saying she felt exactly like Betsy Trotwood in *David Copperfield*, scaring away donkeys in her back garden.

Hours later I was walking past Facey's tent when Gabby called me in; she pointed towards a line of eleven different-coloured pairs of shoes lying in the corner of the tent. She was laughing in deep shock; she couldn't believe that one person owned that many shoes. Facey had basically brought the whole of her bedroom over to Africa. She had made her tent look beautiful with all her creams on the shelves and beads hanging up on the walls, all of which matched each pastel-shaded pair of shoes. Nearly every day she was a different colour.

Facey caught on very quickly to everyday camp life and started working as hard as everyone else. She insisted that she sewed up all the holes in our clothes, and as she sewed she told us all about the Second World War and how much she loved it. She was young at the time and found it terribly exciting, which we all found very surprising. She told us how she had met our grandfather Anthony Nicholls when they both acted in a play called *Vanity Fair* based on the novel by Thackeray. Tragically he died of a heart attack when my mother was twenty-three. I wish I had met him. Travers came in to listen to Facey's fascinating stories, carrying a pair of ripped trousers.

'Granny, can you please sew this hole up?' he asked, at which point she went ballistic.

'You either call me Facey or Faith, you know how I hate to be called Gran, Granny or Grandma.'

One day Mum asked her to help at school and Faith told us the background to Shakespeare's sonnets. This may sound very boring but she made it inspiring.

I was very surprised to hear that 'Shall I compare thee to a summer's day' was in fact written to a man, Shakespeare's patron. Faith is an actress and read the poems lucidly.

After her first week we all noticed that she was blooming out of herself. She was bouncing around, full of life, cooking puddings for us kids and drinking Amarula with Mum late into the night. When it was time for her to go Pieter took her aside and said goodbye to her in private. We all noticed when he came back his eyes were watering.

It was such a shame to say goodbye to my grandmother. She stood in the doorway of the plane with *no* walking stick in her hand and waving with the other. She had left her stick for Oakley to use as a hockey stick, she said she didn't need it anymore. She turned and walked on to the plane… with no wobble whatsoever.

Saying goodbye to Facey left us very sad since we thought it would be a long time until we saw her again; as well as Facey we were missing our sister.

Emily left us in 1996 from the Mission House to start her trip around the world; bravely she travelled alone, and although we couldn't bear the thought of her leaving, we admired her courage. After numerous adventures, she settled in England to start a new life of her own studying Psychology at university and living in a house in London with her boyfriend Jimmy.

One Maun trip with Mum and Oakley a few months ago something happened which took us completely by surprise. We had gone to town to shop and pick up gas. Arriving around lunchtime, we stopped off at our favourite café. Julian's café has undoubtedly the best meals in Maun; he trained at Pru Leith's, his food not only tastes good but also always looks beautiful and he makes the most gourmet banana smoothies. While we were waiting for our food Mum popped into Ensign Services to collect the mail. Ensign is an office service for people in Maun and very useful for those who live in the bush and have no means of communication. Penny, Tracy and Ally have been so kind to us from the day we first arrived in Maun and have supported Mum through some difficult times, and they have also been patient with our unreliable flow of money. When Mum came back she was very distressed. She had received an urgent message to ring Emily but she hadn't been able to get through. This worried us hugely and, abandoning our lunch, we went to ring her father Peter Bourke.

He was bursting and, as he is hopeless at keeping secrets, blurted out: 'Emily has wonderful news but I can't say any more because she has to tell you yourself.'

When Mum told me my heart started to race and my mind jumped to ludicrous conclusions. At last we got through, and a few seconds after Emily answered the phone Mum burst into tears. I knew it. Emily was pregnant. Mum asked her a million questions: 'When's it due?' and 'How did you do it?' – she quickly corrected herself on that one – and 'How are you feeling?' It was due in May. Oakley was ecstatic and all we wanted to do was talk to her. Finally it was my turn. The only thing I could think of to say were 'I'm so excited and happy for you,' but in my delight I was lost for words. Then Jimmy came on the phone; all he wanted to know was how each of us felt. Emily and Jimmy have known each other since they were fifteen. Jimmy has loved her all that time although he never told her till six years later. Now they are deeply in love. I knew this when I first saw them together as a couple.

We couldn't wait to tell Travers, Angus and Pieter back in camp. Mum bought a bottle of French champagne, and Oakley proudly bought his first long-sleeved shirt and tie to celebrate that he was going to be an uncle. The journey back to camp felt like eternity. Halfway home we came upon Inferno, one of Mum's favourite lions. Hugely moved, Mum leaned out of the window and let him know she was going to be a grandmother. We followed him along the road for a couple of kilometres until he moved off. At last we were approaching camp. Trying to keep steady we ambled out of the car but the boys noticed we were beaming with pleasure and, as soon as they saw Oakley's shirt and tie, they asked what was going on. Oakley in his angelic way said, 'Oh, nothing,' and cracked open the champagne. He is only seven and can open a bottle of champagne without spilling a drop.

Finally Mum called everyone to the table. She got to the point; 'Well the reason why Oakley has a tie on tonight is because he is going to be an uncle.' Mum looked around the table, and saw a lot of surprised and confused faces. It took a while, but at last they got it. 'Wow, that's wonderful,' beamed Angus. Travers broke into a sublime smile. Mum and I told them everything we knew and we all thought of Ems, so far away, as we drank a toast to the newest member of our family. Mum felt desperate to be missing Emily's pregnancy and that night we all agreed that we would go back to England for the birth.

I felt exhilarated. For the past year I had been aware that I had been missing England, more than just missing 'home'. Living in Africa has made me see how much I took for granted when I lived in the Cotswolds. Now when I visit England I swim in lakes hidden in a forest, bike for miles on country lanes with my cousin Matilda and notice little details on walks like sparrows, robins and blackbirds. When I lived in England things like that didn't interest me, but now I appreciate them since I don't have to be scared of crocs in the lakes or lions in the forests.

I also miss my English friends. During the last five years I have kept in touch with them all; like any other person, my friends mean a lot to me. I don't understand why some of them haven't come out here. Are they scared? There's no need to be. Some of my friends say they don't have enough money, but maybe they don't need the things they think they need for Africa: khaki safari outfits, hundreds of cans of insect repellent, binoculars, good cameras, the list goes on… All they need is a ticket – simple! They would find lots of familiar things here, for when we left Hollybush we made sure we brought parts of it with us and have made camp as much like home as the home we left behind.

I have also been longing for my dad, and once again Mum and I found another one of our solutions; from now on I will spend three months of the year with my father and nine months at home. This makes me feel settled. Saying

goodbyes to Dad have never been easy because I have not known when I am to see him again. Now I do. This is also a great opportunity for me to get to know my stepmother better. My dad and Cindy Franke have been together for about three years now and are living in Los Angeles.

Cindy definitely hasn't forgotten what it's like to be a child. She has a bubbly personality and is great fun to be with. Even though this is a big cliché it's so true: all you have to do is take one look at her and you know she's a lovely person. Dad and Cindy are perfect for each other. They have the same kind of humour, and that really is incredible, as Dad has such a rare kind. Cindy's got a wonderful smile and sparkly cat's eyes full of energy. When Dad's with her he looks relaxed and contented.

Although I miss Dad deeply I have Pieter in my everyday life so I feel stable. I am lucky to have such kind step-parents. I feel so glad that both of my parents have found love again. Mum and Pieter have been together for four years now and, wonderfully, have decided to get married.

It's quite ironic how Mum, the one who said she would never love another man, is now going to marry Pieter. This news is no surprise to us kids but apparently a great surprise to them. They told us one sunny afternoon on the bank of an island on the Gomoti River. Before going to find lions, Mum and Pieter stopped off at the river and said they wanted to tell us something. I had a clear idea of what was going on and so did Trav. Mum had on countless occasions taken each of us aside and asked,

'What would you think if Pieter and I got married – not that we are.' We had all answered with,

'We'd love it: you know we love Pieter and couldn't think of anything more wonderful.'

As soon as we arrived at the river, we tumbled out of the car, eager to know what was going on. We sat down on the crisp grass in the sun, pelicans flew high above our heads, and we listened to the echoing seagull-like call of the fish eagle; soon we were all ready,

'Well… um… your mother and I have decided to get married,' was the 'unexpected' announcement from Pieter. We asked when and where, and they said they wanted to do it in England.

It seems that all my worries are being solved; we are going back to England for Christmas 2000, and I am going to see my father. We are going to spend two months there, but I will stay on an extra month, as arranged. Unfortunately Mum and Pieter can't get married in England. Mum wanted to get married out in the open, standing in a field with all of their eight children, but unfortunately they could only get married in a church or a hotel. They both decided that they would rather get married outdoors, on an African plain, after they get back from our English Christmas.

This is not just a quick visit, but a very special one. It is the first time in five years that we will be home all together as a family. I love Africa, but we want to keep in touch with our Hollybush childhood. Going back to England is going to be one of the best things for us in so many different ways; Mum and Pieter are going partly to find funding for the lion research project. We kids are going to see our dad, who Travers has not seen for two years. For the first time we are going to see Pieter's mum, our stepgrandmother Moosie. Pieter is going to meet our friends and relatives. And last but definitely not least, we will see Facey again.

Stupid things that are just like everyday life to you will make us all excited: going up stairs, feeling secure in a house made of thick old stone that won't blow down (one Boxing Day my tent in camp was destroyed by a hurricane force wind and I lost a lot of my stuff), being able to press a button on the TV and not having to set up the complicated solar power system we have in camp. Being able to telephone our friends without having to drive two hours to town. It's like going backwards in time; tomorrow we will be driving twelve hours through the Kalahari Desert retracing our steps back to our old, though very different, home.

In a few days we will be walking through the front door of Hollybush, and everything that seemed so big when I was seven may now be small.

A LION'S STRUGGLE
FOR SURVIVAL
TRAVERS

A GUN IS FIRED. Startled antelopes look up from their grazing as the noise echoes across the savanna. As the reverberation fades, one of Africa's most incredible animals struggles to take his last breath through his punctured lungs. All is quiet apart from the sound of the hunter's footsteps on the brittle grass. He squats by the blood-stained carcass, still holding his gun, and smiles as his picture is taken. Victory shots are fired into the air as the proud hunter gets into the car, driven by his guide, and goes back to the hunting camp where he is served a meal and a stiff drink. The skinners then get to work carefully removing the tawny coat from the carcass. Vultures circle above the mass of meat and, as the last car leaves, they descend and finish off what the hunter has left behind.

One of the most magnificent male lions in our study area has just been killed. Armagnac will soon be flown halfway across the world, where on arrival his head will be stuffed and mounted on the hunter's wall, along with the photograph. His skin will be used as a carpet, and the hunter will tell his friends about his trip to Africa, with a few embellishments. Above him Armagnac will stare into oblivion with his new glass eyes.

The hunter saw Armagnac merely as a means to prove his manhood, to us he was source of constant fascination. He was a particularly interesting lion, and we learned a lot about adult male behaviour from him. He was also Courvoisier's coalition partner, and this lion felt his loss even more bitterly than we did.

The first time we saw Armagnac and Courvoisier was on a hot summer's day in 1998. We had been tracking the Santawani pride for quite a while, when at last Oakley spotted Medoc (Medoc and Montrachet were the Santawani pride males at this time). He was lying in the shade with Amarula, a female in oestrus (see Lion Fact File). The other seven females were eating giraffe a hundred metres away. The young cubs were in a playful mood climbing up on to the carcass and jumping off on to the aggravated mothers. We drove towards the inviting shade of a nearby acacia to watch the hungry lions devour their meal. After a while Mum noticed two large male lions lying in the shadows. This was very puzzling, as we would have expected to find only Montrachet with Medoc.

We drove carefully up to the males and to our amazement found they were strangers to us and presumably to the pride. Bafflingly, all the Santawani lions seemed unconcerned by the presence of the two intruders. We spent half an hour noting down their whisker patterns; all the while the cubs played, the females chewed nonchalantly on the carcass, and Medoc continued dozing alongside Amarula. The lions lay beneath a cerulean sky, and the only sound was of flies buzzing round the carcass.

As the afternoon drew on Armagnac and Courvoisier stirred and ambled slowly towards the giraffe, at which point the idyllic scene was destroyed and all hell broke loose. The females immediately sprang up and rushed towards the intruders, deep roars emitting from their chests, their eyes yellowing with rage. Mum hastily wound up Oakley's window, at the same time warning him that the females that he loved so much might soon get very hurt. We knew we could do nothing to stop that and had to let nature take its course. The females surrounded Armagnac and Courvoisier and within seconds were upon them. Two females were tossed high into the air, while the males moaned in agony as the remaining females slapped and bit relentlessly. Meanwhile Medoc was observing the battle from a distance and all twenty cubs, guarded by a pregnant female, were watching intently from behind the giraffe's ribcage. For a minute the air was filled with snarling and high-pitched roars and the lions formed a blur of confusion. Medoc only took action when the males managed to escape the grip of the seven females. He trotted after them roaring and fussing and looking in all directions.

Anxiously we looked at the females through binoculars, and remarkably found they were unhurt. Medoc continued roaring in the distance, and gradually the females moved back to continue their interrupted meal. The stench of the carcass hung heavy in the air; the cubs had stopped playing and dispersed under shady bushes where they lay flicking the flies off their bodies with their tails. A breeze stirred the trees above them and all was peaceful. If we had arrived at that moment we would never have guessed that only minutes before, these tranquil lions had been involved in an aggressive conflict.

We thought that Armagnac and Courvoisier had learned their lesson, but we were wrong. A month later we found almost the whole Santawani pride on a buffalo kill. We immediately recognised Montrachet, Medoc's laid-back partner, and naturally assumed that the other male eating alongside him was Medoc. But when we looked closer, it proved to be none other than *Armagnac*! We couldn't believe it; here was a pride male, with his females and cubs, sharing a buffalo with an adult male lion that was unknown to him. Everyone was very relaxed and no aggression was shown, which was so unlike the last encounter.

When most of the meat had been eaten, the females and cubs walked off, leaving Montrachet and Armagnac eating side by side. As the sun went down, both males walked off in opposite directions, without a snarl or growl. We were fascinated by this and can only assume it to be strategic behaviour. A fight among lions is a very risky business that can result in serious wounds or even death. So it is greatly in a lion's interest to avoid a fight if possible; Montrachet had to weigh up the situation. He was older than Medoc and not as strong and, as there was plenty of meat to go round, sharing was his best option. But this did not explain the females' behaviour; why were they happy to eat beside a strange male in the presence of their cubs? This was partially answered some months later when the hormone results from the poop samples came back. At the time of the fight by the giraffe kill, some of the females with young cubs were in oestrous. At such times they will aggressively resist potential sexual advances by the males, because females can't afford to get pregnant while they still have dependent young cubs. However, on the buffalo kill none of the females were in oestrous.

Do you now understand why we found Armagnac and Courvoisier so fascinating? We learned so much watching these encounters. The notion that pride males ferociously protect their females and cubs from all other males is simply not true. Time and again we have seen lions peacefully or strategically interacting with each other. Aggression is by no means the only form of communication for these intelligent animals.

Over the next year we followed Armagnac and Courvoisier as they roamed through several pride territories, mating when the opportunity arose, on one occasion with a Santawani female. Finally they found four nomadic females and settled down in a corner of the Santawani pride territory. Three and a half months later we were overjoyed to find that two of these females had given birth to cubs. It was around this time that Armagnac was shot. From then on Courvoisier was very shy and we only had sporadic sightings of him with the females and cubs. But he soon disappeared. Courvoisier and Armagnac's little territory was the centre of a great deal of male activity, which was extremely dangerous for a single male on his own.

With the disappearance of their males, the females and cubs were left to fend for themselves. The last time Mum saw two of the cubs was, oddly enough, with Medoc. The females were relaxed in his presence, which she found riveting because Medoc was not the father of the cubs. However the cubs have not been seen since.

This story is still unfolding and recently we were fascinated to see that Courvoisier had joined up with a slightly younger male in the Mogogelo area. Is

this the beginning of a new coalition? We can be sure of nothing at this time, apart from one thing, with a single bullet the hunter changed the course of many lions' lives.

Once lions walked free across vast tracts of our planet. Bit by bit their world became constricted as man drove them off the land and killed them. Living lions had no value then, they merely posed a threat to man's survival. Dead lions proved courage, as they were killed by spears and machetes. The relentless killing of large predators goes on to this day.

The current healthy lion population in Botswana is not only being depleted by trophy hunters but also by farmers. The Wildlife Department has a section known as 'Problem Animal Control' (PAC). The PAC officers act as arbitrators between farmers and the wild animals. It is their job to assess whether an animal is truly a threat to human life, livestock or crops, and if it is, to destroy it. Our experience is that they are extremely reluctant to shoot an animal unless a good case is presented to them. The farmers, however, will shoot a predator at the slightest provocation.

Their visions are very different. The Wildlife Department sees wild animals as a profitable way forward for Botswana, while the farmers see only the value of their cattle. In Botswana cattle have tremendous traditional value and are a way of life for many people. From an early age young children are sent to cattle posts, miles away from their villages, to look after their parents' herds. They are brought up to protect the cows ferociously, and risk a beating if they lose a member of the herd. Cows provide food for the family and pay for a bride. A family's wealth is defined by how many cows they have and it will take a long time for people's priorities to change.

However, large numbers of cattle roaming the land is very destructive. In an arid environment they rapidly drain the grazing resources, leaving very little for other species. The number of cows in Botswana has risen dramatically since European countries encouraged Botswana to develop its cattle industry. This programme was intended to help the people financially, because up until the 1960s Botswana was the poorest African nation. But it proved to be short-sighted as land that was once used for wildlife was laid aside for cattle. The conflict between livestock and predators escalated.

Just think the next time you eat a beefburger, the beef in your burger might have come from a Botswana cow, and a lion may have been shot to protect it.

A fence went up to separate the livestock and game, because buffaloes carry foot and mouth disease and it was too costly to risk the cows contracting it. Fencing the Okavango Delta was a massive operation, the equivalent to fencing a small country. In those early days the buffalo fence killed thousands of wildebeest, zebra and other species, because they were caught in the wire that lay in the way of their migration routes.

In other places the fence has been beneficial as it defines which areas are put aside for wildlife. But that definition is blurred because farmers living in designated wildlife areas hold on to the right to have donkeys, goats, chickens and dogs living alongside them in their villages. This is a serious problem.

In two villages near us three lions have been killed as problem animals. One of the females was a study lion and was shot by a farmer for killing a goat. Domestic animals are easy prey for lions, and even if livestock is put away in enclosures at night, there is a risk that it will be attacked. In that same village one of the Santawani sub-adult males was shot for eating a donkey.

Kilometres away in a village on the boarder of the Moremi game reserve some villagers butchered a female lion. A few days before they had found a dead elephant close to home and decided to collect meat from it. The meat was hacked off the carcass and hung in trees throughout the village to dry. As you can imagine, the smell attracted predators. The female lion came into the village at night and was barked at by several dogs, which she promptly killed, with probably no more than the swipe of her paw. The next morning the incident was reported to Problem Animal Control in Maun but they could not come out because it was Christmas Eve. The villagers took matters into their own hands and set about tracking the female, armed with shot guns, axes and machetes. They found her, but with the crude weapons they could not kill her efficiently. She was badly wounded, and during the fight she leaped upon one of her attackers, mauling him severely, he was flown to Maun hospital immediately amid much anxiety. The lioness was killed. It was later discovered that she was lactating and had several cubs in a den nearby. The cubs died of starvation.

It is asking for trouble for livestock to be allowed to live in designated wildlife areas. People cannot have it both ways; there is no need for a blurred definition, lions should be safe from man on their side of the fence.

Lions struggle to survive in a natural world that knows no mercy. Deaths from natural causes far outweigh those induced by man. In the study area over the last five years we have lost ten adult males in their prime, six adult females and fifty-two cubs, all due to natural causes. They died from disease, fights, being kicked or gored by their prey, from neglect, other predators, broken limbs and old age. Nature has no concept of right or wrong; life in the wilderness is tough and the strongest, cleverest, healthiest, luckiest and most tenacious individuals survive. Sometimes watching nature at work can be very painful.

My favourite lion was Zinfandel. She had a pink spotty nose, a gentle expression, a large muscular body and a shoulder blade that had once been broken and now stuck up just beneath her tawny fur. She was relaxed, elegant and strong and I think the other pride females relied on her; she would take care of the cubs for days on end without irritation while the rest of the mothers went off by themselves. One afternoon we found her dead. I was devastated. There was nothing left of her except a mangled collar, which had been chewed by hyenas, and Zinfandel's black tail tip, which I keep in my tent. The tail tip and collar were lying near a zebra carcass that she presumably took part in killing. The zebra probably lashed out with its powerful back legs as it was being attacked, inflicting the fatal wound; we will never know.

I have been talking a lot about death: hunting, problem-animal and natural deaths. However, the most important thing is life and the value of living lions. Living lions challenge us, when we see them we look beyond their beauty and get in touch with our most ancient fear. Fear played a large part in our ancestors' lives and enabled their survival. Clearly they did not get eaten by lions and must have used their intelligence to outwit them. Curious people can now come to Africa and watch lions reasonably safely, and while doing so they can explore their deepest past. This is an emotional experience that has great financial value. The future for Botswana and its lions lies in tourism; the country's mineral wealth is a fickle commodity and will eventually run out. Lions have the potential to last forever as long as they are ferociously protected. By this I do not mean interference; they can solve their own problems brilliantly and creatively given the space and freedom. However, there is one problem they cannot resolve, being shot.

In the year 2000 the hunting trophy quota was thirty adult males, of which nineteen were killed. A conservative estimate is that an additional one hundred male and female lions, of all ages, were shot as problem animals. If Botswana is to maintain its healthy lion population, this cannot go on. Mum and Pieter have appealed to the government for a total ban on lion trophy hunting. This request is not based on sentiment but on hard scientific facts and a comparison with other African countries where lions have been over-hunted and populations decimated. We still have an enormous amount to learn from this highly complex and intelligent species and the only way we can do that is to defend these last few populations.

Who do we put first: ourselves or the lions? Are we going to set aside certain corners of the earth for wildlife to roam free and with confidence? Will we be generous enough to give them what they need or will we force them to struggle on, whatever the consequences may be? I know how I feel.

Wherever you are in the world tonight, look up into the night sky and know that somewhere out there, across the wide open spaces, there is a lion walking free and safe across the African savanna, roaring into the distance.

ION FACT FILE

The information in this fact file
has been gathered from observations
made over the last five years.
We have been lucky enough to live
in a research camp and to be allowed
to share in Mum and Pieter's work.
We would like to thank them both for
giving us permission to use their data,
some of which is being published here
for the first time.

They have let us be part of the research
and as a result we have learned to think
about what we see. There are still many
questions left unanswered and years
of research to come.

The Pride

Female lions define the pride. A pride is made up of a group of adult females and their cubs. While some of the females may be related to each other as mothers, daughters, sisters, aunts and cousins, others will not be genetically related. The number of lions in a pride fluctuates as cubs die and young adults leave. The number of breeding adult females in our study prides ranges between three and eight. Larger prides have been recorded.

Females inherit and roam large territorial ranges, in our study area the average size of a territory is about 300 square kilometres. Neighbouring pride territories overlap at times due to the movement of prey animals, and we have seen dynamic shifts in territorial ranges over the years. Females with cubs may vacate vast areas of their territory to avoid confrontations with strange males. Mum and Pieter are still studying these territorial fluctuations, but we can all see that territorial boundaries are fluid.

A pride male is an adult lion that the females will both mate with and tolerate around the cubs. However, as you will see, the pride male is by no means always the father of the cubs (even though he thinks he is). A pride can have from one to seven pride males. In our study area we have never seen more than four and most prides have two pride males. Pride males remain with the females for a period of time (known as their tenure) that

can last from one to six years. Longer tenures have been recorded.

Pride members do not always stick together and it can take months to learn which lions form a particular pride. We think the best way to explore a pride is to start at the beginning of a lion's life.

Cubs

When they are born, cubs are tiny (about 1.5 kg), blind and blue eyed. Female lions have a very short pregnancy, only 110 days. As a result, the cubs are born defenceless. They cannot walk and are covered in light brown spots to help camouflage them from many predators. Male and female cubs are the same size at this point in their lives. An adult female may give birth to anything up to five cubs, however the death rate in the first few weeks of life is high and litter sizes range from one to four cubs.

Dens

Females temporarily leave the pride to give birth. They do this alone in dens. These are usually in dense scrub, forests or virtually impenetrable, low-lying acacia bushes known as Lion Bush. Dens are enclosed and females are highly defensive; as a result the cubs have contact only with their mothers during their first six weeks. However, we do see other pride members pay visits to the den sites, and they sometimes remain close by for several days.

Mothers leave their dens for several reasons: to hunt, to mix with other pride members, to be alone. Interestingly, we have seen denning females mate with non-pride males during the brief oestrus peak that follows birth (see Oestrus and Infanticide). These trips away from their cubs can last from a matter of a few hours to anything up to five days. Cubs left for prolonged

Like all mammals, female lions undergo rapid hormonal changes after giving birth, and at this time they are acutely sensitive. Stress may impact on milk production. It is thought that females often move their dens, but this is unlikely to be true because the journey puts the cubs at risk. Females only move their dens in the first six weeks if they are under pressure or threat. In two years we have only seen one female move her den during those early weeks.

Joining the Pride

Six to eight weeks after giving birth, the mother leads her cubs from the den and joins the rest of the pride. Females with cubs of similar ages will link up and share the suckling. This makes it very hard to know which cubs belong to which mother, as they all suck from whichever female is in the mood. At times females are not very tolerant of the cubs. During these early days the cubs familiarise themselves with other pride members (both relatives and non-relatives), and in the case of female lions these bonds may last a lifetime.

periods get very emaciated and look awful but soon recover once they start sucking again. It is possible to assess whether a female has recently suckled by looking for a dark brown ring around her nipples; the ring slowly fades over time if she has not suckled.

The cubs stay in the den for six to eight weeks and are totally dependent on their mother's milk; therefore we do not visit the den site, as it may put the mother under unnecessary pressure.

By now the cubs can walk, run and play, although they are still very clumsy and little more than balls of fluff. We are very careful to be especially quiet at these first sightings of the cubs. It is important that they do not get scared of the research vehicles, as they will be seeing us nearly every day while we watch them growing up.

Maturing and Playing

Cubs grow very slowly in their first year, for, like human babies, most of their early energy is spent on brain development. Lions are highly intelligent animals and, during their time with the pride, cubs have a great deal to absorb. They must learn to groom themselves and each other, to find their way around a large territory and to recognise what is safe to touch or eat; and they must learn how to hunt. They must be aware of predators, and know how to scan the sky for distant vultures that may lead the pride to a free meal. Play forms a huge part of this learning and binds the cubs together, further developing their familiarity with each other.

Cubs start eating meat when they are about three months old, though we have seen hungry cubs sucking on meat at eight weeks old. Cubs are weaned when they are between five and ten months old. This wide variation is dependent on the tolerance of the females and availability of prey, but on average cubs are mainly eating meat at eight months old. We have noticed that the cubs that suck for a long time seem to look healthier.

Males and Cubs

It is assumed that males play a large role in the bringing up and protection of cubs, but from what we have seen this is not always the case. We have seen pride males tolerate the presence of strange males near their females and the cubs, and it is not unusual for pride males to abandon a pride while the cubs are still dependent.

Pride males have no reliable way of knowing which of the cubs are theirs; indeed they have no means of knowing if they are the fathers at all (see Oestrus and Mating).

When the cubs are small the pride males are tolerant of them, indeed we have seen females leave their seven-month-old cubs in the care of the males for several days. Small cubs do not eat much meat therefore the males sense no competition as they devour a carcass; male lions are highly competitive when they are eating, and can be aggressive. But as the cubs get older and require more food, the males become tetchy and less tolerant. No more allowances are made for the growing cubs and it is not unusual to see them looking very skinny at times.

Growing up and Leaving the Pride

Due to their slow early growth, at one year old cubs are the size of a Labrador dog. However, during the following eighteen months rapid growth takes place and the males start to develop some scruffy little manes. They also grow significantly bigger than the young females, and it gets easier to tell the sexes apart. During this time the cubs remain highly dependent on their mothers.

The cubs now start to take a much more active interest in hunting, however they are still inexperienced and get overexcited. They often run at the prey too early and ruin the hunt.

Between eighteen months and two years the young lions' testosterone and oestrogen levels are rising. Testosterone and oestrogen are both reproductive hormones and are produced by the body at higher levels as the young lions start to develop. At this time we see them start to explore their sexuality and engage in play-mounting with pride members of any sex. They are becoming aware of the power of their reproductive hormones and are constantly sniffing each others' and the adult females' genitals. Sometimes they can become quite frenzied if oestrogen levels are high in pride members.

Oestrogen sends out strong sexual messages and both attracts the males and triggers the females to want to mate. This is a period of confusion for the young lions; we have seen a young male mount his sister (they came from the same litter) but they only coupled for seconds. The youngsters even try to mount the adult females that are in oestrus and are quickly pushed off.

At two and a half to three years the young lions, or sub-adults as they are now known, are quite big; the males are the size of an adult female. They have learned how to hunt, scavenge and how to protect themselves. They are now capable of leaving the group, however some prefer to stay in the protection of the pride. The adult females can be very intolerant of both male and female sub-adults at this time. The adult females are now responsive to mating again and start to break off from the group to seek mating opportunities. Often the young lions are left in the care of one adult female, who finds herself stuck with the responsibility of monitoring the still inexperienced sub-adults; as a result her next litter is delayed.

If new adult males try to take over the pride at this time the sub-adults can be at significant risk. The females

are still too young to mate and therefore of no interest to the new males, and adult males are always aggressive towards unfamiliar young males. The adult female will move her charges to a peripheral area of the territory to avoid confrontation with the new males. However, sooner or later these as yet non-reproductive sub-adults will be forced to undergo a perilous and challenging journey; they have entered their nomadic phase.

The Nomadic Phase

The nomadic phase is a testing and dangerous time for young lions, as for the first time in their lives they have to function independently of adults. The young lions of both sexes leave their natal pride (the pride they were born into) together; this group is called a cohort. Initially the young lions remain within the familiar pride territory and occasionally link up with the pride females for short periods. Young nomadic lions may form brief associations with other nomads of similar age.

After a while the cohort splits up, and males and females go their separate ways. Why is this? Natural selection will have worked against lions that mated with close relatives, and it may also have acted against breeding among lions that have been brought up together. The males' long, tough nomadic phase is a big test of their survival skills and natural selection is at work again.

The nomadic phase is complex and we need to look at males and females separately.

Nomadic Females

Females inherit their territorial range and where possible will stay in their natal pride territory. The nomadic phase enables the young lions to develop further their formidable hunting skills. We have seen two young females bring down an adult zebra. The skills they develop at this time will help these young lions raise cubs of their own. Females do not always give birth at the same time and some will have to raise cubs initially without the support of other pride members. We have seen several females do this and the harsh nomadic phase has given them the opportunity to learn the necessary survival skills.

Young sub-adult females undergo a shorter nomadic phase than males because at three and a half and four years old they are old enough to mate. On reaching sexual maturity they either rejoin their natal pride, as they will now be tolerated by the new pride males, form a satellite pride of their own or in some cases we think they may link up with neighbouring prides they have associated with in the past. Mum and Pieter are currently investigating this intriguing possibility.

Nomadic females still require a great deal of research, but from observations these females seem to have fewer aggressive encounters with other lions than their male counterparts.

Nomadic Males

Young males are extremely reluctant to leave their pride and their familiar pride territory. But there are several factors that cause them to move out of the area. First, the males are now so big that they can dominate the adult females at kills; as a result the females become increasingly intolerant of their company. The young males spend less and less time with their mothers, but still remain within the familiar pride territory; they know the area inside out and feel safe.

Second, when new pride males come into the area, they are extremely aggressive to any sub-adults they find in the territory. When they encounter such young males they can injure them badly, sometimes even killing them. However the sub-adults can still be strongly reluctant to leave, we have seen many young males stick around despite dreadful injuries. However, the intolerance of adult females coupled with the aggression of adult males finally add up to a serious amount of pressure on the young lions.

It is at this point that migratory prey animals, like buffaloes and zebras, may influence the young males' movements. Such large herds are so tempting that they may follow them out of the pride territory and thereby start to explore a wider world. It will be at least three years, however, before they are strong enough to take over a pride of their own.

The years ahead are dangerous because the young nomads will now be moving through other pride territories. The resident pride males or even the females may attack them. (Though we have seen groups of strange sub-adults tolerated by females in our study prides and sharing at kills. Lions are by no means as aggressive as people think and will often behave co-operatively even with strangers.) It is not only lion attacks that cause death; occasionally prey animals deal a mortal blow with a hoof or a horn. But perhaps more worryingly, these non-territorial males are often seen at the edges of wildlife areas where they encounter their greatest enemy, man. Human settlements where cattle and donkeys roam free provide easy pickings for lions, and the young lions are often shot as problem animals.

Many males that leave in a cohort do not survive. If their numbers have been brought down to one or two their chances of taking over a pride are small. The remaining males then join up with other nomadic males. This new grouping is called a coalition.

Some males undergo a second semi-nomadic phase. Females with cubs are intolerant to mating, and males will explore neighbouring territories for more receptive females. This exploration can take them far from the pride territory, and they may abandon the pride. Adult males that

have been pushed out by new males, once again roam pride territories, mating when the opportunity arises. On occasion, these older males link up with a younger male and may attempt their second pride takeover. We have seen several older males move into a pride and reproduce.

Reaching Maturity

A male lion has reached his adult body size at six years old, although his mane will continue to grow. He is awesomely strong and is now ready to try to take over a pride with his coalition partners. However there are no guarantees that this will be successful and some may die in the attempt. Some males remain nomadic and mate when they get the chance, as described by Travers in Chapter 5. Others will become pride males. Pieter and Mum are still investigating why they do that because, as we will explain, not all the cubs in a pride are fathered by the pride male. To be able to understand this we need first to look at females and how they reproduce.

Females

While males come and go, most females stay put inside their territory (for exceptions see Nomadic Females). The females do not necessarily spend all their time around each other. Groups can change from day to day and week to week. Some females prefer to be alone most of the time, and only join their pride mates when they have young cubs.

While some females are closely related (mothers, daughters, grandmothers and sisters), other females in the pride are less related (cousins and second cousins) and some are not related at all. Females form links that last a lifetime because they live around one another. How related the adult females are depends on whether their fathers were related. Not all coalitions are formed by related males, added to that we see that pride males are not solely responsible for fathering cubs. If non-related males have fathered the cubs for several generations, relatedness between some females can be very dilute. (However, a coalition of related males

can somewhat restore the balance over the next generation.) This is a complicated issue and is covered brilliantly in Pieter's book *Prides*.

Lions are the only social cats and there are many practical reasons why they form close bonds. Females share suckling and take care of each other's cubs. By banding together, they can pull down large prey such as buffalo and giraffe, which would be virtually impossible for a single female. We have also observed another behaviour that may motivate females to stick together. Females with dependent cubs need to avoid pregnancy until their cubs can fend for themselves. A group of adult females is a daunting defence against pride males or nomadic males who want to mate with them against their wishes.

Oestrus

Females are happy to be mated when they are between three and a half and four years old, however they will have started to have oestrus cycles before this time. Like domestic cats, female lions are induced ovulators. This means they require the stimulus of mating to release their mature eggs. Like other cats, lions are continually producing eggs. When some of her eggs are close to maturity, oestrogen levels rise, the female goes into oestrus and is ready to be mated. If she is not mated the unreleased eggs just disintegrate. Oestrus lasts between four and six days. When she is in oestrus she has hormones in her pee that make her very attractive to males. Lions are always smelling each other's pee. When they sniff pee with higher levels of oestrogen in it than normal, males (and females) are triggered to make a grimace that is called 'flehmen'.

The hormonal message in a female's pee tells a male she is ready to mate; it also makes him want to mate. As we spend so much time with the lions we can tell if a female is coming into oestrus by watching for flehmen, as well as looking at sexual behaviour between them, like mounting. On average, females 'cycle' every sixteen days but there is a lot of individual variation. Females that spend a lot of time together seem to come into oestrus at the same time.

It has long been believed that after giving birth a female does not go into oestrus until her cubs are between eighteen months and two years old. However, after years of observation and poop sampling, Mum has shown that this is not the case. On average, females resume normal cycles six months after their cubs are born. But like human females there is considerable individual variation. Some females resume cycles within two months, while their cubs are still sucking. Females in oestrus can be very irritable with their cubs.

Cycling females with cubs avoid mating either by moving to the outskirts of their territory or by being highly aggressive towards the males. We have witnessed pride males attempt to mate oestrual females with cubs and have seen many facial wounds inflicted by intolerant females upon these frustrated males.

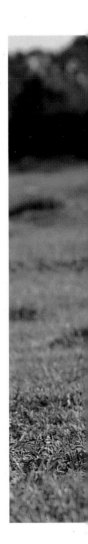

Like domestic cats, female lions have brief oestrogen peaks just before they give birth and just after. At this time the females are attractive to the males though the female is reluctant to mate. On several occasions we have seen mating take place during the latter part of pregnancy and once just after cubs were born. This is highly significant (see Infanticide).

Mating

We have watched a lot of lions mating. They mate for days at a time. (They can take so long we have to bring picnics in the car and sometimes we spend all night with them and sleep in the car.) As we have said, females need to be mated to make them release their eggs. The male can mate with her as often as every fifteen minutes for anything up to five days. But sometimes this energy is wasted, because not all mating results in pregnancy. If a male comes upon a female too early in her oestrus and starts mating before her eggs are fully mature, it is going to take the female longer to release her eggs. By the time she does, it is likely that he will not have any sperm left.

We often see two males present at matings. It seems that the first male to find the female in oestrus gets the chance to mate. The other male just hangs around, sleeping under a nearby tree. Maybe he is being very clever, because we often see the females leave the male she has been mating with for a long time and sneak off to the other

male. Sometimes she mates with him; if his sperm count is fresh and high he can fertilise her, he will probably be the father, and the other male will have done all the work necessary to cause her to ovulate.

We have seen brief encounters between a mating pair, lasting a matter of one to two days, result in pregnancy. In these cases the male has encountered the female in the middle of her oestrus. Given the opportunity, a female will mate with more than one partner during her oestrus. Recently we witnessed Krystal mate with her pride male on one day and the following day we found her with a pride male from a neighbouring territory. We look forward to finding out who fathered the cubs that are currently in their den. Pieter and Mum will do this by collecting tiny skin samples, using a dart shot from an air gun. The DNA taken from the cub's skin will tell us who the father is. The prick from the dart is no more than that of a thorn and the sample only has to be done once.

Pride Males

Trying to take over a pride is very difficult, and can be extremely dangerous. A small coalition or cohort will seek out a pride with weak or old pride males or, better still, be lucky enough find a pride of females that have been abandoned by the previous pride males. A larger coalition or cohort (three to six males) may take over a pride using brute strength to push out healthy males. In our study area we have never seen coalitions with more than four males, and most coalitions are formed by two males.

Aggression

The risks in a pride takeover are great to both the resident males and the incoming males. The incoming males can hang around sussing things out for many months before they make a move. It is assumed that male lions are highly aggressive in their behaviour. We have found this not to be true on many occasions. There is an important difference between an animal being driven by aggression and being capable of aggression; the first is instinctive and the second requires thought.

Their great power enables lions to inflict terrible wounds on each other; this is costly and wherever possible they will try to avoid combat. We have witnessed males chasing each other but not attacking, and avoiding violence by being submissive. Most nights we hear them roaring to warn off other males. However, in five years we have only witnessed one death caused by violence, when a single male encountered two large males in the night. None of these males were in their own territory and the victim was bitten twice through the chest puncturing his lungs. The aggressors lay peacefully 50 metres away from him and moved off that night with no further violence. The single male died hours later. This is not to say that males do not fight, we have seen some very serious wounds and some lions have gone missing, presumed dead. But it is clear that lions can be strategic and different lions make different choices.

Infanticide

Males do commit infanticide (the killing of a young cub by an adult) though Mum and Pieter believe it is not an automatic response for new males to kill any cubs they see. Infanticide has rarely been witnessed; yet often the disappearance of cubs is assumed to be the result of infanticide. As the carcasses are rapidly devoured by scavengers, the cause of death cannot be determined. Have the cubs died from disease, been left unprotected by their mothers, been killed by predators or have they been killed by an incoming male? If so, what motivates some males to kill cubs?

It is a well-established fact that males of any species do not want to waste their time bringing up a strange male's offspring. There is only one way that a male lion can be certain he is not the father, if he has *never* mated with the female he sees with the cubs. Under these circumstances he will commit infanticide.

Yet, as we have said, male lions can roam in and out of pride territories for months and even years before they settle down. During this time they encounter pride females and mate when they have the chance. Even a brief mating in the past will persuade him that he is the father of any cubs that he sees with that female in the future, and as a result he will not kill them. Lions are clever but they cannot calculate the length of a pregnancy.

It was thought that because females

rarely give birth until their previous cubs are between eighteen and twenty-four months old that they simply did not return to oestrus until this time. Therefore, by committing infanticide, males encourage the females back into oestrus; but by looking at hormone levels in poop samples, Mum has shown that, like other cats, female lions come back into oestrus soon after having given birth.

Nevertheless, the female reproductive system may provide a subtle means by which females can cuckold, or trick, males into believing that they are the fathers of the cubs and thereby defend them against infanticide. Because a pregnant female has an oestrogen peak before giving birth, an incoming male that comes across her assumes she is in oestrus because she smells right and mates with her, albeit briefly, as she is reluctant to mate for long. We have witnessed such matings and the cubs have later been accepted by the incoming male as his own.

Females also have an oestrogen peak after giving birth, which is characteristic of most induced ovulators. (For species with rapidly maturing young it enables the females to become pregnant again as soon as possible.) This peak provides female lions with another means to deceive incoming males. We have witnessed this form of cuckoldery with Sauvignon, a female from the Santawani pride.

She was made pregnant by Medoc, the pride male at the time, but during her pregnancy he was chased off by two new males, Fouleur and Ferriere. They became the new Santawani pride males and have since mated with the females. Soon after the arrival of the new males, Sauvignon had her cubs. It is possible that Sauvignon had encountered Fouleur and Ferriere before, as they had been seen in the area. However we were worried for the cubs when we found Fouleur near the den site for several days after Sauvignon had given birth. Was he going to commit infanticide? Days later we were amazed to find Sauvignon mating with Fouleur for a period of five days. This was full-on mating, not flirting behaviour, and she mated with Ferriere on the fifth day of her oestrus. During this time she left her cubs and did not suckle, the brown rings around her nipples faded until they almost vanished. Two days later we found her reunited with her cubs, they were thin but sucking once more.

Medoc and Sauvignon's cubs have since been accepted by Fouleur and Ferriere as their own. This an example of how the relatedness between cubs in separate litters can be diluted.

We think it is important to stress that incoming males are not automatically driven to kill any cub they see and will only kill cubs if during their lifetime they have never encountered and mated the female before. Another cause of death of young cubs can be indirect infanticide caused by female neglect. The presence of incoming males can be stressful to the females and negatively influence their behaviour towards their cubs. Another form of indirect infanticide can be the result of poor maternal care and inexperience. Remember that Lancon, the mother of the 'insect' mentioned by Maisie in Chapter 3, was careless enough to lose her cub, which later died. Lions lead complicated lives and it is hard to predict their behaviour.

Taking Possession of the Pride

We have seen some fascinating behaviour after a takeover. Some females can be very flirtatious but at the same time resist mating. Others will mate for very extended periods, but, as mentioned in the section on mating, if one male dominates a female throughout the whole of her oestrus, he will not be able to maintain sperm production and therefore will fail to fertilise her when she finally ovulates. Some males put more pressure on the females than others and follow them around relentlessly for months. Others use an altogether different tactic and are much more deferential. In the early days of Medoc and Montrachet's tenure of the Santawani Pride we were amused to see them politely standing back at kills and allowing the females to feed, but this good behaviour did not last long.

Having successfully laid claim to the females the males then have to learn their new territory and patrol it vigorously. They must learn where prey is available in the wet season and, in the dry season, where the nearest water is. And most importantly they must defend the territory from incoming males. Pride males can hold on to a pride for anything between one to six years (longer than this has been recorded). Sometimes they choose to leave once the cubs are around a year old, as the females are still not happy to mate again with dependent cubs to raise. Abandoning the pride is a risky strategy for the males as it leaves their adopted territory undefended, yet access to more willing females elsewhere is a tempting prospect, and males rarely pass up the opportunity. For a pride male life is fraught with risks and uncertainties. And in spite of all their hard work they have no guarantees of paternity. It is our personal belief that male lions have harder lives than the females.

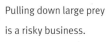

Pulling down large prey

is a risky business.

Hunting and Scavenging

Mostly, when lions are in a large group, they will hunt large prey, like buffalo and giraffe. When they are in a smaller group or by themselves, they hunt small animals, such as warthog and impala. Lions usually hunt at night, under cover of darkness. However lions don't always obey these rules.

You would think that the Mogogelo pride, with six females, eight big cubs and two pride males would hunt huge animals, but they don't. This pride lives by permanent water and hunts throughout the daylight hours, killing small animals regularly. On the other hand the Santawani pride, who live mostly in forest, hunt at night, they prefer large prey and have become expert at killing giraffe.

Lions are not very reliable hunters; we have often seen hunts fail. Scavenging provides them with an easy meal, as they have no trouble chasing off other predators from their kills. We have seen them a number of times looking up into the sky and noticing vultures circling kilometres away. The lions, that have been looking so lazy in the sun one minute, spring up and run arrow straight to find cheetahs, Wild Dogs or leopards on a kill. No one dares to stand up to a lion and those that do more often than not get killed. Lions have very sharp eyes and also very sharp ears.

One day we were having breakfast

when a pack of Wild Dogs burst into camp and killed an impala right in front of our eyes. It seemed like only moments later when Claret, Krystal and Cinsault, three sub-adult lions we knew well, came dashing in and stole the kill. It was remarkable that the lions (having been two kilometres away) had heard the kill.

Seeing a kill is upsetting and gruesome. We haven't seen many kills, as we leave the lions in peace to hunt, but when we do it's very shocking. We have seen how much time and effort it takes to pull down large prey, and how risky it is. We now realise why lions scavenge so much.

Lions are very opportunistic hunters and one of the things that we have been interested in is the huge range of diet that the cats have. As well as the usual selection of prey, such as impala, zebra, warthog, etc., we have seen them eating small birds, spring-hares, ostrich, aardvark and honey badgers, and attempting to kill porcupines. The most remarkable sighting we have had was Medoc cracking open six ostrich eggs, slurping up the yolk and eating the live chicks.

Christmas 2000 on our visit back to Hollybush.

ACKNOWLEDGEMENTS

WE WOULD LIKE TO THANK the Government of Botswana for allowing us to live in their country, and the Office of the President for granting Mum and Pieter research permission and thereby giving us the opportunity to live in the bush and work closely with lions. We would like to thank the Botswana Department of Wildlife and National Parks for giving us children support and encouragement. With special thanks to Dan Mughogho, Lucas Rutina, Ma Panyane, Mandy, Madipa, Marokane, Moremi, Dimana, Madongo, Philemon, Simon, Colin, and Scar.

THE SANKUYU COMMUNITY for allowing us to live on their land. Crocodile Camp Safaris, most particularly Karl-Heinz Gimpel for his unfailing loyalty and support to Mum and Pieter and for allowing our family the privilege to set up camp near Gomoti Camp. We would also like to thank Desmond Green for his friendship and help. A very special thank you goes to Corrie Smuts-Steyn for kindly donating his magnificent wildlife and bush photographs. Corrie's love of the lions and support for our project is unfailing and we will always be grateful to him and his wife Anne.

HOLLYBUSH: We want to thank Rose Rawlins for looking after us so beautifully when we were babies and young children, and Harold Mennel for looking after Hollybush and keeping it like home for us to come back to. Our grandmother Facey and David Woollard for sorting out problems in Hollybush, helping to raise funds, coping with any crisis without fail but most of all for their love, humour and kindness. Our friends Polly and Jenny, Chris Jefferies and our neighbours Greg and Lorna. Chrissy, Bonnie Jack, Ruskin and Joseph; and our family in England, the Sturriges, the Mallinson's, the Judges for staying loving and loyal in spite of long separation.

MAUN AND FRIENDS: Thanks to Ally, Penny, Tracey, and Kay at Ensign Office Services for their love, support and unfailing loyalty, also thanks to Ester. Patrick Akhiwu and Allison Brown for taking care of us. Roddy and Sue Bateman at the Land Rover dealers for selling us excellent cars and keeping them on the road. Special thank you to Wessel for even coming out to the bush to fix our cars. Stanley and Paul at Spar, who have been very patient with us. Johan and Annelies of Drumbeat safaris for kindly giving us access to their office and computer. The Penstone family Patrick, Heather, Julian and Penelope for their friendship, good food (and thanks from Mum and Pieter for the good wine!). All those at Riley's Garage, who have helped us on many occasions. Gametrackers Botswana for allowing us to get drinking water from Santawani. Thanks to all those at Women Against Rape, particularly Irene Fergus and Anne Sandenberg, the pioneering work continues to help women and children in Botswana. To all at the Thuso Rehabilitation Centre, whose imaginative and creative work helps disabled and handicapped people and their families to live independent lives. The Lutheran Day care Centre for AIDs orphans, who provide counselling and support and a constantly open door to anyone who needs their help, most particularly, thanks to brave Stella and Mr & Mrs Sorenson. Hilda from the Faroe Isles, who showed us human tragedy, courage and triumph, she opened our eyes and our hearts. Her house was full of love and became home-from-home to our family. Mel, Ken and Shereen Oak for advice and wonderful homemade jam.

THANKS TO THE SANDENBERG DYNASTY: Anne for her untiring support during our difficult early days; Peter, Mandy, who opened their house to us and supported us at all times; thank you to Peter for a wonderful Christmas at Delta Camp and to the children Jethro, Baz and Zora for their friendship. John, Vivian, Jake and Emma for their friendship and sports equipment. David, Alain and Damien. Hazel Wilmot for her awesome generosity; without her support, life in the early days would have been far more difficult. David and Roger Dugmore at Kalahari Kavango for their guidance, advice, generosity and two wonderful safaris. Katherine and Ralph Bousfield and all at Jack's Camp. Brett Saunders, David Sandenberg and Gremlin for allowing us to stay at Jungle Juction on the Zambezi river. Dougie and Sandy of Grey Matters, and their elephants, Marula, Jabu and Timbi for taking us on the ultimate bush walk. Sandy, Ruth, Lena and her mother Karen Ross for being Maisie's second family. The Leavers: Eric, Joan, Carrie and Jessica.

THE LONGDEN FAMILY: Tim, Bryony, Maxime, Pia and Blythe for taking us under their wing when we first came to Botswana and for giving us their lifelong friendship. The Kohlers, Reiner, Birgit, Sebastian, Phaia and Emily for their generosity and friendship. Dave, Jasmine, Adrian and Matthew for giving Travers and Angus a welcoming home in Maun at anytime. Ian Cunningham Ross, Steve, Nookie, Tammy, Pamela, Laurence, Helmut, Hannelore, Nicole, Florian, Anna, Miriam and Ellinor, for their friendship. Teachers Andrew Hepburn-Brown and Karen Dooley for helping and advising Mum in the early days of home schooling.

WE WOULD LIKE TO THANK the many people in Maun who have helped and supported us in many different ways, there are too many to list and we are lucky to live in such a close and friendly community

CAMP: Our thanks to Olivia (Kelly), Gabby, Nafatse and Bring for looking after our family so beautifully. Their loyalty, friendship and companionship will never be forgotten. Kate Evans and Sophie Greatwood for their affection and commitment. Cathy Zerbe, though she lives in town, is part of our life in camp and needs a very big thank you, as a friend and teacher she is simply the best.

PROJECT: Thanks to Steve and Sally Kendall for buying the project a much-needed digital video camera, Vodafone Group Plc and Globalstar Southern Africa (Pty) Ltd for donating a satellite phone and to all at The Born Free Foundation for taking the project under their wing and helping us to raise funds and awareness; also for being so friendly and kind to Mum and Pieter.

BOOK: We would like to thank our agent Georgina Capel for her enthusiasm, fairness and her trust in taking on such young writers, she has become a friend to our family. Also, Anita Land, Robert Caskie and Yvonne Anderson at Capel and Land. We have Georgina to thank for giving us the privilege of working with an editor as great as Philippa Brewster. Her care, guidance, patience and skill have helped us become better writers and we own her a life long debt of gratitude. Not many editors would be prepared to edit in the African bush, while putting out bush fires and coping with marauding elephants waking her up in the night. Not many editors work with three inexperienced authors at the same time, she gave each of us the opportunity to find our own way through the editing process and showed us the value of professionalism. She too has become a great friend of our family.

WE WILL ALWAYS BE ESPECIALLY INDEBTED to Anthony Cheetham of Orion who showed great courage by believing in child authors. He has changed our lives and we hope one day that we can repay him. We are grateful to all at Orion for looking after us and helping us through the complex process of getting a book ready for publication, especially Trevor Dolby, who is always there to answer our many questions and never fails to be anything but positive and helpful, and Pandora White.

IT IS ALMOST IMPOSSIBLE TO DESCRIBE the gratitude we feel towards Richard and Lalla Dawkins. We received Richard's first letter of support for our book on Christmas Eve 1999. Without Richard and Lalla this book may never have been published, for it was they who gave the incomplete manuscript to Georgina and started this incredible journey. Juliet Dawkins read the early drafts and made some very helpful suggestions, Lalla, who is an artist, encouraged Maisie with her drawings; in fact the whole Dawkins family have given us the confidence and encouragement we needed to struggle on when things got tough. Richard has been kind enough to read all the drafts and has always made useful and incisive comments, we have learned a great deal from him.

WE WOULD LIKE TO GIVE VERY SPECIAL THANKS to Emily for being a phenomenal sister, a constant support and for helping to bring us up; she is a huge part of our lives and of this book. Oakley Purchase for his wonderful contributions to the book that have lit up the story, and to our step-sister Philippa Kat.

LASTLY, WE WOULD LIKE TO THANK our Dad and Cindy, Mum and Pieter for their help, love and commitment and Pieter for letting us use some of his photographs. Dad read all drafts, made many excellent suggestions and spent days helping us choose the photographs. His artistic eye, attention to detail, care and patience have been invaluable. Mum and Pieter have lived and breathed the book for the last year; they have encouraged and supported us through the whole thing. We cannot begin to thank them enough, without them it would not have been possible.

Anyone who is interested in finding out more about the Okavango Lion Conservation Project or making a donation can contact The Born Free Foundation on:

TEL: 01403 240170

WEB: www.bornfree.org.uk

E-MAIL: wildlife@bornfree.org.uk

BORN FREE FOUNDATION
3, Grove House,
Foundry Lane, Horsham,
West Sussex, RH13 5PL

INDEX